Kathy's new book, *The Grin Gal's Guide to Wellbeing:* great resource for any woman looking to improve physical and spiritual fitness. What makes the practical support she offers so powerful is that she dedicates sections to prayer and Bible study in every single chapter. Truly, a faith and fitness lifestyle is incomplete without these. Instead of presenting wellbeing as an ideal lifestyle to attain, she drives a better perspective—that God calls all of us to a life of stewardship. Get the book for yourself and a friend, not because you want to do fitness better, but because you want to be the light of Christ for yourself and others.

—**Brad Bloom,** publisher, *Faith & Fitness Magazine,* faithandfitness.net

As someone who has been maintaining a 100+ pound weight loss for many years and today runs the Faithful Finish Lines online weight-loss program, allow me to encourage you to read this book. Kathy writes with heart, clarity, and compassion about the struggles we face as we attempt to follow God's directions in taking care of our physical, mental, and emotional health. What I love about Kathy's perspective is that she weaves God's voice and the wisdom of scriptural truth into every section of the book. Plus, she brings her delightful sense of humor into the mix so that you'll walk away feeling encouraged and refreshed. I will be recommending a copy to women who work with me.

—**Sara Borgstede,** owner, Faithful Finish Lines (Christian weight-loss programs for women), author of *Fear Less: 30 Devotions for Courageous Faith,* www.theholymess.com

The Grin Gal's Guide to Wellbeing goes beyond typical weight-loss programs. It identifies where you're stuck or struggling and helps you trust God to care for your soul and cultivate wellness in your physical, emotional, and spiritual life. Kathy Carlton Willis has extended our work in our book, *Journey of the Soul,* to promote your soul care and overall health. With each page, you'll find inspiring stories and Scripture meditations, practical exercises, and laughs to lift your spirit!

—**Drs. Bill and Kristi Gaultiere**, psychologist (Bill) and therapist (Kristi), church ministry, founders of Soul Shepherding and authors of *Journey of the Soul: A Practical Guide to Emotional and Spiritual Growth*

Take a tip from a do-as-I-say, not-as-I-do surgeon. Embrace the principles of *The Grin Gal's Guide to Wellbeing.* Kathy Carlton Willis explores healthy lifestyle changes from a holistic, Christian worldview. The Grin Gal's heartwarming stories, practical homework, and heavenly insights will inspire you to grin on the inside. Everyone struggling with wise health choices needs to digest Kathy's practical insights in their journey to wellness and wholeness.

—**Charles W. Page MD, FACS**. Dr. Chuck is a speaker, author, surgeon, TV show host, "bush-hogger," and father of five fabulous children. charleswpage.com

The Grin Gal's Guide to Wellbeing is well laid out with thought-provoking chapters. If you were to ask me to write a book from owning a CrossFit gym for eleven years, then this would be the book I would write. Incredible! I love how it addresses the motive of having a wellbeing focus for God's glory. This guide reflects my heart and soul. It handles fitness correctly and helps produce biblical wellness that's actually sustainable for life. Kathy Carlton Willis truly nurtures the body, soul, and spirit. I'm not only inspired to keep moving but to look deeper at my "whys." The book ends with resource chapters relevant for putting into practice what Kathy effectively empowers you to do!

—**Trey and Stephanie Curtis**, co-owners of Be Challenged Community Gym (formerly Cross Fit), hosts for church fitness small group; (Trey) bachelors in church ministries and MA in counseling, LPC/MFT, certified personal trainer from National Academy of Sports Medicine.

As a certified Wellcoach® and life purpose coach, I know to take care of our bodies we must focus on improving the health of our minds, souls, and spirits, as well. Kathy's book speaks to me in fresh and new ways to connect with my inner being. It motivates readers to set goals that nurture and rejuvenate every aspect of wellbeing. One of the ideas that stood out to me was her recommendation to go on a worry fast. Her emphasis on walking away from legalism to find wholeness also resonated with me. *The Grin Gal's Guide to Wellbeing* is a must for every woman who desires to be healthy and fit inside and out as a way to bring honor to God.

—**Crystal Breaux**, BS in kinesiology/corporate fitness, certified Christian life purpose and Wellcoach®, V.P. of Created Woman, former weight management and fitness instructor

I'm a huge fan of *The Grin Gal's Guide to Wellbeing.* It's a perfect mix of inspiration and practical information to help motivate and support readers on their wellness journey. As a wellness professional and a Christian, I love Kathy's focus on the Word of God as foundational to making real progress in our lifestyle goals. A healthy life is one that encompasses our mind, body, and spirit, and the author does a fantastic job of balancing all three. She offers a holistic approach to wellness that is unique in the health and fitness industry and so refreshing! I especially enjoyed her emphasis on "soul-care" over "self-care," a commonly misunderstood element of wellbeing. If you've ever struggled with guilt for making yourself a priority, then this book will help you overcome that mindset and move forward with freedom and joy. I highly recommend this book to anyone ready to make positive changes in their mind, body, and spirit!

—**Karen Ferguson**, content creator, health coach, and the author of *Breath of Life: Living God's Promise of Peace in the 7 Dimensions of Wellness,* www.karenferg.com

I'm a practical person, so I gravitate to stories that not only inspire me but also grab my hand and show me an attainable path. That's exactly the tone of Kathy Carlton Willis's new book *The Grin Gal's Guide to Wellbeing.* Her immediate connection as a fellow struggler on the whole lifetime search for balanced health put me at ease and helped open my mind and heart to the specific suggestions she made with each entry. This is a book to not just read but to work through and experience—which is how any transformation occurs. I found the chapter prompts especially helpful: Heartstrings (stories), Help Me! (tools), Heavenly Insight (Bible), Homework (dig in), Health Check (evaluation), Hurrahs and Happy Dances (celebration), and Hope Quest (prayer). If you're ready to do the work, let the Grin Gal take your hand.

—**Lucinda Secrest McDowell**, award-winning author of *Soul Strong* and *Life-Giving Choices,* www.LucindaSecrestMcDowell.com

As a board-certified life coach, specializing in trauma-informed modalities, I know firsthand how women are seeking emotional health and wellbeing. In her new book, *The Grin Gal's Guide to Wellbeing*, Kathy Carlton Willis speaks from her own story of healing in hopes of guiding and leading readers in their stories of healing. With authenticity, truth, and a whole lot of love, Kathy helps each of us smile broadly in an unrestrained manner!

—**Janell M. Rardon**, MA, author, founder, The Heartlift Practice, www.janellrardon.com Trauma-informed Therapist, Certified Aroma Freedom Practitioner (AFT)

The Grin Gal's Guide to Wellbeing has tips, hacks, advice, and examples for everyone—no matter where you are on your wellbeing journey. Whether you're searching for physical or mental health development, this book touches all the corners of well-rounded health. One of the sections that resonates with me personally is "Those Dreaded Plateaus." Reading this chapter made me feel as if someone related to me—an accountability partner helping me through unsure times. With my background in healthcare and as a former certified personal trainer, I highly recommend this book for overall balance in body, soul, and spirit.

—**Sarah Wisor Martinez,** neurosurgery senior clinical research coordinator, MA in public health, former personal fitness trainer and water aerobics instructor

I highly recommend *The Grin Gal's Guide to Wellbeing* for those seeking practical and spiritual steps in personal growth and wellbeing. Kathy takes self-care to a new level that digs deep to the root issues of our souls. This book made me feel seen by the author, that she related to my life. Kathy's biblical approach to wellness has inspired me and left me wanting more!

—**Carli Graves**, barre instructor, dance teacher, 18 years of dance experience and 3 years of ministry experience

As a psychotherapist, I found *The Grin Gal's Guide to Wellbeing* to be a practical resource. I appreciate Kathy's approach of combining sensible strategies for health with biblical truths to create an overall plan for wellbeing. My clients will benefit from the tools and motivational insights Kathy provides based on her own experiences of working through roadblocks to live a healthier life.

—**Cassandra DeWall**, licensed professional counselor at Praise Church, helping clients achieve a healthier mental outlook, specializing in anxiety disorders and transitional life stages/events

The GRIN GAL'S GUIDE to WELLBEING

Being Well in Body, Soul & Spirit

To Your WellBeing ☺

Kathy Carlton Willis

Kathy Carlton Willis

3G BOOKS

The Grin Gal's Guide to Wellbeing: Being Well in Body, Soul & Spirit

www.kathycarltonwillis.com

ISBN-13: 978-1-7330728-4-7

Published by 3G Books, Beaumont, TX 77706

www.threegbooks.com

Editing, interior, and cover design by Michelle Rayburn www.missionandmedia.com

Contents

INTRODUCTION

At first glance, you might think this is another Christian weight-loss book, but that isn't the primary focus. As I began my own physical wellbeing program, I realized the importance of also caring for my soul and spirit. "Don't you realize that your body is the temple of the Holy Spirit, who lives in you and was given to you by God? You do not belong to yourself, for God bought you with a high price. So you must honor God with your body" 1 Corinthians 6:19-20. In an attempt to take care of the temple, I determined the dweller of the temple needed even more attention—that invisible part of me and God's Spirit in me. So in this book, you'll find an emphasis on wellness, wellbeing, and wholeness that goes from the inside out. My story started with wanting to lose some weight. Maybe that's where you're at too. Or maybe you want to put personal stewardship into practice. Stick with me for a few chapters, and we'll integrate body, soul, and spirit.

The hardest exercise I ever tackled

I grew up skinny. I really did. I was still underweight when I married my high school sweetheart. But soon, the pounds found me. A few snuck up on me because the food budget allowed for unhealthy choices easier than healthy choices. And I'm sure as I entered my twenties, my metabolism changed.

When I started my first diet, my beginning weight was the exact number I hope to get to as my goal weight now! And I thought I was heavy.

Over the last thirty-plus years, I've fought through multiple medical diagnoses, more than twenty surgeries, and nearly annual rounds of physical therapy and rehab due to injuries and setbacks. The unfavorable outcome on the scale worsened with hundreds of different prescriptions. Each new medical challenge caused me to gain more weight.

Fast-forward to my fifties. I was one hundred pounds above my so-called "heavy" weight when I graduated from college.

Every pound robbed me of more and more vigor—of life. And as my cells slowed down, the scale increased. I felt like a slug. A slug that experienced pain each time I tried to budge a muscle. Unhealthy food choices introduced me to diabetes.

But all that changed when I faced the hardest exercise I ever tackled. It wasn't in a fitness center or with a weight-loss group. It wasn't with a group class. This exercise didn't cause me to sweat—well, maybe it did.

The hardest exercise I ever tackled was determining to get up and do something—anything—to not allow my situation to get any worse.

Until the "want to" is engaged, the ability to make healthy choices will never be permanent. It might last for a while, like a fad or a trend. But soon, the old ways will creep back in. It's more convenient to do what you know than to pursue a new way of living. Doing the right things in life requires challenge, discipline, focus, determination, and willpower. But without a growing intimacy with Jesus, all well-meaning intentions are powerless.

Maybe some of you are in a similar predicament. You've put on more weight than you thought possible. You've fought medical challenges that complicated your pursuit of health. Giving in to a sluggish metabolism has caused you to purchase clothing in larger sizes. The easy diets you went on in your early adult years no longer work. I get it. It's no picnic!

This book is a result of my own quest for wellbeing—being well. During the pursuit to find improved health, better looks, and more energy, I discovered wellbeing is more than physical wholeness. It's a balance of body, soul, and spirit.

The Grin Gal's Guide to Wellbeing is not just about my weight -oss and wellness journey. It's a guide to help others in pursuit of wellness find their own answers. And those answers will not be identical to mine. I'll share what I've discovered, but your discovery will be different—just as God created you to be different. You're unique, so your plan, program, and process will be unique to you.

I'll share details about how I'm seeing victory despite dealing with a bunch of challenges. I've lost and fifty pounds and maintained that weight for five years. I'm on my "weigh" to losing more. This book offers honesty, humor, and occasionally, homework!

Note: I realize some of you have irreversible conditions that will only recover with a God-given miracle. I'm not promising that all your health problems will go away. But what I'm saying is that we can all experience better body/soul/spirit wellbeing, and in doing so, we might see an improvement in being well too! Oftentimes, it's a reduced intensity of a physical symptom or an improved mindset that gets us through the day.

Without a growing intimacy with Jesus, all well-meaning intentions are powerless.

I believe God wants each of us to do those things within our means to be healthy, such as eating good nutrition and getting exercise. He also wants us to occupy our minds with what is good and virtuous instead of what makes us feel defeated and discouraged. By taking an active, educated part in our wellbeing, we will show God we're willing to be responsible to take care of the resources he's given to us and in us—personal stewardship.

For groups and individuals

This program is ideal to do on your own or in a group. I'm offering a free downloadable leader's guide on my website if you want to lead a group through these materials.

www.kathycarltonwillis.com

Besides this book, a quarterly planner is available to help you stay on track. When our Wellbeing Warriors focus group went through the book materials, they noted how handy a habit tracker would be to plan their intentions and track their progress. They were tired of having multiple planners to juggle for different aspects of their lives. Enter *The Grin Gal's Planner for WellBeing: A 90-Day Habit Tracker for Being Well in Body, Soul & Spirit.* When you use this book and the planner together, you are equipped to make real progress. See back of book for more details, including sample pages from the planner.

Navigate the book

Each chapter will include the following:

- Heartstrings (Stories)
- Help Me! (Tools for Equipping)
- Heavenly Insights (Bible Study)
- Homework (Making it Real)
- Health Check (Evaluation for Body/Soul/Spirit)
- Hurrahs and Happy Dances (Celebration of Victories)
- Hope Quest (Prayers)

What qualifies me to write this book?

I have asked myself several times why I think I should write this book since I have not "arrived" in a place of 100 percent success. I do have a strong background on this topic. And while I haven't completed all my goals, the invitation for you to join me in the journey is timely. God's Word is the authority, and I'm just a co-traveler with you. But in case you want to know my life experience with wellness of body, soul, and spirit, here are my credentials:

- Wrote a college research paper on Christian aerobics.
- Earned two degrees: Bible and church education. The college granted me the Key Award.
- Took college and continuing-ed classes in counseling, anger management, and other courses related to soul health.
- Trained for and led First Place groups and Fit 4 groups.
- Am a Bible study leader and writer.
- Worked for three different physicians as assistant. Medical terminology is my second language.
- Trained as a fitness buff for competitions in my twenties.
- Led fitness classes at several different churches.
- Am on the journey to wellbeing with you.

What others are saying

For a year now, I've interacted with a group of women in a Wellbeing Warriors focus group. They have provided feedback as I provided each chapter of material and each resource. When you go through this book, you become a Wellbeing Warrior too!

I asked these gals to provide input on how this book was valuable to them. This is what they said:

- Is adaptable for wherever you find yourself in the effort to take care of yourself.
- Shows me there's no need to be perfect to start caring for myself.
- Includes thought-provoking questions.
- Gives practical tips, tools, and takeaways to make positive changes to daily routines.
- Provides tried-and-true methods supported by Scripture.
- Helps me learn the difference between soul and spirit and how to care for each.
- Reminds me of my responsibilities regarding personal stewardship, but in a grace-filled, not legalistic, manner.
- Equips with well-rounded applicable solutions for getting out of your own way.
- Speaks with an authentic voice of experience, providing an appealing sisterly feel rather than that of an overly perky cheerleader or bold infomercial motivator.
- Reflects a come-alongside (me-too) attitude. Inspires a "we're in this together" spirit.

The dilemmas

During my wellbeing journey, I've had to deal with a few unexpected situations. You might face similar dilemmas or different ones unique to you. Be ready! Look at them as simply success signs that you are fighting the fight of being a Wellbeing Warrior.

If you have much weight to lose and the pounds start creeping off, you might receive the accusing tones of others. Sometimes it's hard for them to be happy for you, so they find ways to discount what you're doing. I've had plenty ask me if I "had help" with my weight loss. By help, they mean, did I have surgery for it. I didn't, but they implied my victory against the excess pounds didn't count if I did!

Another dilemma I faced was when I got under two hundred pounds. Many of us who have a lot to lose call this "onederland." I wanted to announce my arrival to onderland on social media, but

I struggled with the sense of shame to admit how heavy I was at my starting weight. I decided a victory is a victory, and there shouldn't be shame or stigma attached to it. So, we had a great celebration!

Many of the Wellbeing Warriors mentioned the battle of participating in family traditions involving food. It's an individual decision about which dishes to eat and what portion sizes to choose. Mostly, it's about being present and enjoying those moments without feeling obligated or tempted to partake in the foods not on your plan. Most agree it isn't the food that provides the biggest problem at these family gatherings but usually a sabotaging family member. This book will help you be prepared. Also, there are times it's a perfectly acceptable plan to eat off-plan.

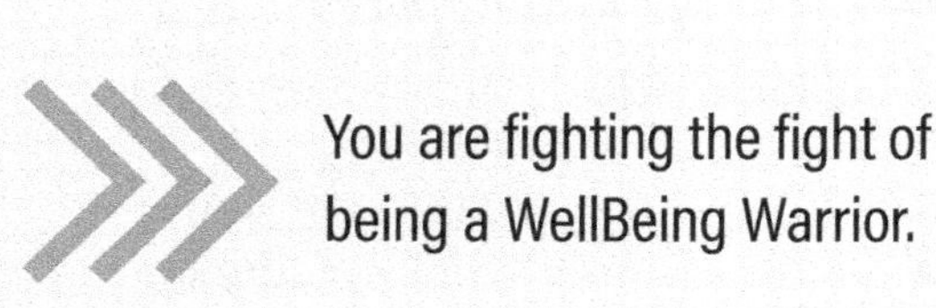

Dilemmas provide an opportunity for us to experience the victory of making wise choices as well as the occasion to speak up regarding the happiness of being on the wellbeing journey.

The terrible toos

Since I love doing everything with a grin, I thought I'd close out this introduction with a *Grin Gal* story to tickle your funny bones.

Let me set the scene. I was invited to be the keynote banquet speaker for the prestigious Write-to-Publish Christian writers conference. The seats were filled with writers and colleagues. Literary agents and acquisitions editors I esteem as the best of the best attended. I was pretty sure a couple of the ones sitting in the crowd were undecided if they liked me or not. My presentation for the night was about overcoming excuses, titled "The Terrible Toos."

Well, evidently, when you speak on "The Terrible Toos," you're qualified to be the expert on the topic by having a *too* funny (or *too* humiliating) moment right before you speak. Not once, not twice, but three times. The outfit I wore seemed to fit when I tried it on a couple of weeks before the trip. But when I dressed in my dorm room, I realized the skirt had nearly non-stretchy elastic and I was *too* tiny for the outfit. (Normally when I size out of a garment, it's a reason to celebrate, but not right before a speaking event in said outfit!) Before leaving my room, I did some creative tucking. But after a long walk from dorm to banquet room, I realized the skirt would be going,

going, gone if I didn't do something. So, I borrowed a safety pin from a friend, and others helped secure the offending garment.

The host seated me at the head table. Did the slightly trembling hands reveal my insecurities? Then the audio tech handed me a mic pack for recording purposes and suggested I go ahead and put it on so I wouldn't have to get up again between the meal and the program. When I latched the pack to my waistband, it acted as an anchor, weighing the whole thing down. (And I do mean d-o-w-n.)

I sat with some of my heroes in the industry—it felt like being at the grown-up table. I sensed trouble in waistband land. So, I headed back to the bathroom to tighten the pin. On the way out of the banquet hall, the mic pack unclipped and fell off my skirt onto the floor as a hundred attendees (making two hundred eyes) focused on me. Actually, the incident was hardly noticed, but it *felt* as if I had made a scene. I scooped up the pack, hoisted my skirt to make sure it didn't fall, and scooted to the women's room.

Concerned friends joined me, and we secured the box to the back of my jacket collar and pinned the skirt, *again*. I went back out, acting as if nothing was the matter, and enjoyed the meal and great conversation at my table, soaking it all in. But then I made the mistake of turning in my chair to watch the director honor the awards recipients, and I felt a *boing!* The pin gave way. The pointy end was as good as any alarm going off! Back to the bathroom I ran, knowing I had just minutes before it was time to speak. Friends assisted again. We used pins, tape, anything we could find! This time it held, and I delivered the keynote.

Of course, the example of my wardrobe malfunction (without all this detail) made it into the speech. The keynote went fine (there were some BIG GOD moments in it), but now I know to double check my wardrobe before I pack, not after I have a mic pack!

Benediction

> *May he equip you with all you need for doing his will. May he produce in you, through the power of Jesus Christ, every good thing that is pleasing to him. All glory to him forever and ever! Amen.* (Hebrews 13:21)

YOU NEED A PLAN

Some of us are planners. So, when we hear that this wellbeing thing works if you have a plan, we get excited. But some of you resist plans. They make you feel restrained and constricted. What if I told you that you'll experience the best freedom imaginable while pursuing a plan for health of body, soul, and spirit? Plans don't have to be systems telling you what you can't do. They can be journeys allowing you to explore boundless options leading to a better life. Plans show you what you do best!

Heartstrings

How did you do it?

At the beginning of 2016, I started a self-improvement program that was so successful, I've lost and kept off fifty pounds, have gone off insulin (which doctors said would never happen after being on it so long at such a high dose), and have seen other major health benefits. People assume I underwent weight-loss surgery or endured an unhealthy, wacky diet to get such drastic results. As I write this, I still have more to lose, and we're going to do it together.

You're reading my story because you want to see positive improvements in your own life too. The glory of this plan is that it's customized to your personal set of challenges and desires, with no program to buy.

Some say they don't want to take the time to make the changes necessary to see real progress with wellbeing. Yes, it takes time, but those months are going to come and go whether we make them count or not. Two years from now, if you continue on your current path, what might be the outcome? But if you invest that same two years determined to make choices that are best for your wellbeing, what might happen? You see, if God leaves us here, that two years will tick off on our calendar one way or another. But how we decide to spend those two years can make all the difference in the world. Rather than bemoaning the amount of time it will take to see results, let's flip the switch and be excited that in the near future, our situation can be better than we ever dreamed possible!

If you kicked all your excuses to the curb, what is your heart's desire for wellbeing?

Heavenly Insights

It isn't wise to plan without seeking the wisdom of God and the advisors he has placed in our lives. Wisdom tells us to hold loosely to our plans, knowing they can change in an instant. Instead, we adopt the mindset of "If the Lord wills it, I will . . ." I have found it's powerful to speak the intentions God has placed on my heart. It's best to not have human escape hatches from the plan—yet be content for God to revise the steps of the plan for a better outcome. And there are times as we customize the plan that we adapt it for better productivity. Changing the plan is necessary to improve it, but it isn't a loophole permitting us to escape if the plan gets too hard.

If you spend time with God and seek his heart for your life, he will lead you to create a wellbeing plan for being well. When we take our action steps from his direction, we seek and yield to his control rather than merely asking him to bless our self-made plans.

Commit your actions to the LORD, and your plans will succeed. (Proverbs 16:3)

What is the *why* of your plan?

What actions do you need to commit to the Lord?

What mindset and actions will set you up for success, and which ones will sabotage your results?

May he grant your heart's desires and make all your plans succeed. (Psalm 20:4)

If you kicked all your excuses to the curb, what is your heart's desire for wellbeing and being well?

How will you successfully deal with those things you just kicked to the curb so the trash collector can pick them up and destroy them?

We can make our plans, but the L*ORD determines our steps.* (Proverbs 16:9)

After you tell God your desires, ask him to show you the steps he recommends so you see his desired outcome. What ideas surface?

Invite God to be with you as you take those steps. We are a destination people, but he is a journey God.

Good planning and hard work lead to prosperity, but hasty shortcuts lead to poverty. (Proverbs 21:5)

What shortcuts are you tempted to take?

Why won't these work for the long haul?

How much time and focus will it take you to commit good planning and hard work to wellbeing?

Trust in the Lord with all your heart; do not depend on your own understanding. Seek his will in all you do, and he will show you which path to take. (Proverbs 3:5–6)

Have you trusted the Lord for your wellbeing? What might be holding you back from complete trust?

What is your own understanding telling you that could derail you from this process?

What is God's will concerning your wellbeing?

What path is he showing you to take? You'll know it because it's the one that gives you the most passion and peace.

And so, dear brothers and sisters, I plead with you to give your bodies to God because of all he has done for you. Let them be a living and holy sacrifice—the kind he will find acceptable. This is truly the way to worship him. Don't copy the behavior and customs of this world, but let God transform you into a new person by changing the way you think. Then you will learn to know God's will for you, which is good and pleasing and perfect. (Romans 12:1–2)

How can you look at your wellbeing plan as a living and holy sacrifice?

Why does God find it acceptable?

How is this a way to worship him?

How will the process transform you into a new person: body, soul, and spirit?

What will it take to view and value your plan as good and pleasing and perfect?

Help Me!

What is your why?

All of us have different hopes for wellbeing. It isn't about seeking perfection. Wellbeing is officially defined as "the state of being comfortable, healthy, or happy."[1] Wellbeing integrates mental health, physical health, and spiritual health.

To get to your best requires deliberate effort—being intentional about being well, rather than simply letting life happen to you. The goal for functioning at your optimal condition isn't for vainglory but for God's glory.

When I started, what did I hope *my best* would look like? (Keep in mind your list will be different.)

- Rehabbing injured and inflamed body parts.
- Being the strongest, fittest version of myself possible.
- Reducing the intensity and number of health conditions and medications.
- Looking my best.
- Becoming vital and vibrant.
- Having fewer injuries and illnesses so I could endure a full and fulfilling speaking schedule.
- Enjoying healthy body, soul, and spirit for more ministry moments.

What doesn't work:

- A temporary goal, such as an upcoming event.
- Doing it because someone else is doing it.
- Feeling guilted or shamed into it.

Ready, set, action!

After I addressed my issues and dreamed up my wellbeing goals, I decided on the action steps I'd need to take in order to get to my best self. If you are fighting overwhelm, your plan might need to focus on one thing at a time. Your plan will be different, but here's mine:

- Design an exercise plan to get me from my former state of fitness (or lack of fitness) to my best—staged for success, not for failure.
- Create an eating plan focused on good taste and good nutrition (mostly unprocessed foods in the best balance of macros—good fats, lean proteins, and complex carbohydrates).
- Track my food and fitness faithfully. I use MyFitnessPal.com.
- Devote time to learning good nutrition and exercise. Use what I learn to customize a plan suitable for my challenges and my goals, my likes and dislikes. Consider this a continuing education program rather than one-and-done research.
- Surround myself with positive reinforcements such as cheerleaders, healthy food choices, and fun clothing choices in reduced sizes (from resale shops).
- Spend more on groceries and less on eating out.
- Dress for exercise as soon as I wake so I don't talk myself into not working out.
- Partner with an accountability buddy, reporting in weekly and exploring what is working and what needs to be changed.
- Remind myself this is a quest, not a quick fix. It will take a long time to reverse the effects of my poor eating choices and sedentary lifestyle.

If I can do it, you can too!

Homework

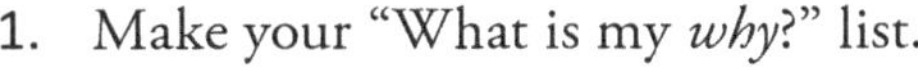

1. Make your "What is my *why*?" list.

2. What struggles have you had this week? List them and brainstorm ways to prevent or overcome them moving forward.

3. Create your initial wellbeing plan.

Health Check

Body: What physical symptom or ailment would I like to improve?

Soul: What does my inner being require to be excited about beginning this plan?

Spirit: How will I connect with God through this process?

We are a destination people, but he is a journey God.

Hurrahs and Happy Dances

List your victories from the week and celebrate them. Share them with one of your cheerleaders. Note any aha! moments from this week.

Hope Quest

Father, I'm celebrating the start of my wellbeing journey, knowing you love me so much and you are with me through the entire process. Continue to equip me with willingness so I'm fueled with purpose for the days ahead.

WHAT'S GOD GOT TO DO WITH IT?

It's difficult to follow God's direction regarding our wellbeing efforts. There are times we're uncertain what steps he is leading us to take. Other times we know the right way to go, but we are resistant to it or too tired to make the effort.

Most of us who follow Christ desire to do what God wants us to do. But when it comes to stepping out of our comfort zone, then we struggle.

- **Faith** = stepping out of our comfort zone and trusting God. (Let's call it the faith zone!)
- **Obedience** = following God's direction, knowing he will do it through us, even when we don't think we can do it. (See Philippians 4:13.)

How do we differentiate between good direction and God's direction? God shows us his direction by giving us certain passions, personalities, ideas, and opportunities. He never guides us astray from his Word and his Spirit.

Heartstrings

As the chapter title asks, what *does* God have to do with our wellbeing? This is certainly not the type of journey we want to embark on by ourselves, even with very well-meaning intentions. We will find too many frustrations along the way unless we make this a lifetime of serving God with our choices. And really, the "how to" for wellbeing comes down to choices, doesn't it?

God is generous when it comes to equipping us with all we need to grow.

There are times when God's Word and Spirit convict us, meaning God shows us the error of our ways. What do we do when the guilt we experience is from God? The best choice is to have true remorse and seek his help to change directions (repentance). Other times guilt is false guilt or residual guilt. We need to know how to differentiate that from God's correction. False guilt is when we are down on ourselves or are feeling fragile. Often that's enough for us to feel defeated. Sometimes Satan shows up to pile on more false guilt. Residual guilt is when we've already confessed our rebellion to God and received his forgiveness, and then we keep revisiting the problem because we can't forgive ourselves or move on. Here is a comforting thought: when we are a child of God, there is no condemnation in Christ Jesus. (Holy Spirit conviction is always with the goal of restoration, not condemnation.)

> *So now there is no condemnation for those who belong to Christ Jesus.*
> (Romans 8:1)

Be assured of this:

> *Don't you see how wonderfully kind, tolerant, and patient God is with you? Does this mean nothing to you? Can't you see that his kindness is intended to turn you from your sin?* (Romans 2:4)

Let's be ready to grow in the area of wellbeing based on God's purpose. When we feel defeated or fragile, what a gift we have to be able to take our wounded hearts to Papa God for reassurance.

Heavenly Insights

> *If you need wisdom, ask our generous God, and he will give it to you. He will not rebuke you for asking. But when you ask him, be sure that your faith is in God alone. Do not waver, for a person with divided loyalty is as unsettled as a*

> *wave of the sea that is blown and tossed by the wind. Such people should not expect to receive anything from the Lord. Their loyalty is divided between God and the world, and they are unstable in everything they do.* (James 1:5–8)

Even if you don't feel as if you have enough wisdom to accomplish what you need for wellbeing, you can ask God to give it to you, and he will bestow knowledge and understanding in your mind and heart without even scolding you.

When you ask for wisdom, ask in faith, believing with unwavering confidence that God will accomplish in you what he wants through this.

God is generous when it comes to equipping us with all we need to grow.

> *For because he himself has suffered when tempted, he is able to help those who are being tempted.* (Hebrews 2:18 ESV)

Jesus is the perfect one for us to come to with our wellbeing struggles because he knows all about suffering when tempted. He is qualified to help us.

What is one thing about your wellbeing struggle that you are afraid to talk to God about?

> *Now may the God of peace—who brought up from the dead our Lord Jesus, the great Shepherd of the sheep, and ratified an eternal covenant with his blood—may he equip you with all you need for doing his will. May he produce in you, through the power of Jesus Christ, every good thing that is pleasing to him. All glory to him forever and ever! Amen.* (Hebrews 13:20–21)

Think about God being a God of peace. How does that help you with your wellbeing?

Think about God having resurrection power. How does that impact your wellbeing priorities?

Think about God being the Great Shepherd. Does this role help you in seeking his will for your body, soul, and spirit? Describe what his shepherding looks like in your pursuit of wellbeing.

All Scripture is inspired by God and is useful to teach us what is true and to make us realize what is wrong in our lives. It corrects us when we are wrong and teaches us to do what is right. God uses it to prepare and equip his people to do every good work. (2 Timothy 3:16–17)

If Scripture is given by God to teach us, how can the Bible help us on our wellbeing journey?

What correction from God's Word have you received lately?

What teaching have you asked God to show you?

What is the ultimate purpose of God's correction and teaching?

Help Me

Don't ask God to bless what *you* want to do, but instead ask him to show you what *he* wants you to do.

We may feel inadequate, unworthy, or unprepared, but God will never abandon us where he leads us. His presence will be with us, and his power will equip us. (See the chapter "Equipped for Wellbeing.")

God (with his divine power, which is superior to our insufficient human power) has given us everything we need to live a godly life of wellbeing.

> *By his divine power, God has given us everything we need for living a godly life. We have received all of this by coming to know him, the one who called us to himself by means of his marvelous glory and excellence.* (2 Peter 1:3)

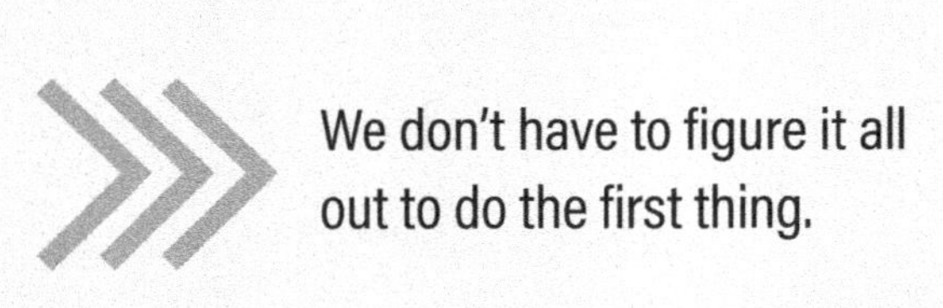

Often, we don't take the first step if we don't know where the path will eventually lead. We fear it might be too hard. The unknown keeps us from doing what we do know. How many times have we heard someone say they are waiting to know God's will before they do anything? The truth is, we already know so many choices that are good for our wellbeing that fit into taking care of the temple and being a good steward (caretaker). We don't have to figure it all out to do the first thing. When our first step is obedience, God will provide "on-the-job training."

When is the best time to work on your wellbeing plan and program? The same time you are doing your devotions and having your quiet time with God. Along with reading your Bible, praying, and worshipping, seek his direction and keep track of the brainstorms God gives you to take care of your body, soul, and spirit. Seeking wellness and wholeness in wellbeing is an act of worship and devotion to Christ.

When you surrender it all to God, you are in the right position for God to bless.

- Work hard. What can you give up or reduce that takes time, energy, and focus away from being all in with your wellbeing?

- Show God your dedication by being a continual learner. He is all about using students who like to grow.
- Write down bits and pieces of ideas that come to you so you can put together a plan for wellbeing of body, soul, and spirit that fits with God's direction.
- Pray about specific goals. Desired outcomes of wellbeing don't just happen.

God uses resources to help equip you. List your resources. Then place a checkmark beside the ones you're using now.

What gets in the way of what you believe God wants you to do with your wellbeing? If we're not careful, whatever gets in the way becomes our little *g* god.

Homework

1. Reword Hebrews 13:20–21 to personalize it with your name.

2. Seek God's wisdom, allowing him to be the vision-caster in your life. List wellbeing steps that you believe are pleasing to God. You won't know all the steps right away. However, journal the ones you do know.

3. What struggles have you had this week? List them and brainstorm ways to prevent or overcome them moving forward.

Health Check

Body: What is one way I rebel against God's direction physically?

Soul: How will I adopt the mind of Christ regarding my wellbeing this week?

Spirit: When will I have a date with God to seek his will for my wellbeing?

Hurrahs and Happy Dances

List your victories from the week and celebrate them. Share them with one of your cheerleaders. Note any aha! moments from this week.

Hope Quest

God—
Show me
Forgive me
Open to me
Teach me
Nourish me
Enable me
Direct me
Supply me
Encourage me
Nurture me

INSIDE OUT

The secret to wellbeing seems to be taking care of our inner selves. Scripture addresses our inner being using several different terms. This chapter will help us sort it out and then learn how to pursue wellbeing where it matters—that part of us that goes to heaven when we die (if we've received Christ's gift of salvation).

I confess to having a hard time with writing this chapter. For every word you see here, I have studied a hundred words on the topic. How do I boil it all down in a succinct way when it's so confusing? This is one of those concepts in which we can have childlike faith, but it's also such a mystery that we never quite grasp the totality of the meaning. And that's okay. Let's explore what we can and leave the rest for later in our journey.

Heartstrings

I remember the first time someone in my extended family passed away. We all descended on the surviving spouse with every manner of casseroles, pies, and flowers. Upon arrival, we little kids ran off to play, unhindered by the weight of grief. Not grasping the finality of it.

When we came in for pie, the grownups shared family memories. Then the photo albums came out, and we heard more stories. Sometimes they cried and laughed in the same sentence. Tissue boxes were scattered around the house. I remember how close the air felt in those grieving rooms. As if I was suffocating.

Then the adults seemed to need cuddles with the young ones and hooked us into their arms. We sat on laps or at their feet. Stroked their crepey skin and gave squeezes at what seemed like appropriate times.

In that moment, I learned about the soul and spirit. Mom prepared me for going to my first funeral. She explained that our bodies are like houses. The part that makes us real—that makes us different from one another—is what lives inside the houses. Mom said when God decides we no longer need to live in our earthly house, he takes us to live in his home in heaven. Since there's no need for our bodies anymore when we go to heaven (only one tenant per house-body), the tradition on earth is to bury the house (the body). But she said not to be sad because the part that is really alive is that invisible part that went to heaven.

When we got to the funeral home, the casket was open, and Mom pointed out that the body wasn't moving anymore because the person no longer lived inside it. *Was it sort of like the shell left behind when a cicada flies away?* Even though we were sad that we couldn't be with our loved one until seeing him again in heaven, we didn't have to be creeped out by his body in the coffin. The box that looked sort of like a bed was the new place for the house-body to rest since our loved one didn't need it anymore.

As I grew, I learned that the inner part of us is known by many terms. Soul. Spirit. Heart. Mind. Will. We will explore these terms further in this chapter and future ones.

Heavenly Insights

Today we are looking at the words *soul* and *spirit* in Scripture. Notice we are examining the lowercase *s* spirit, not the capital *S* Holy Spirit references.

The basic definitions are:

> **Soul:** The mind, emotions, personality, and will (the invisible part of me that makes me who I am).
>
> **Spirit:** The spirit is the only way to communicate with God and grow spiritually.

There are times the Bible seems to reverse the meaning of these terms unless you explore the origin of the words. This is why it's easy to get confused with the definitions. Let's look at some of the key verses.

> *For the word of God is alive and powerful. It is sharper than the sharpest two-edged sword, cutting between soul and spirit, between joint and marrow. It exposes our innermost thoughts and desires.* (Hebrews 4:12)

We know that the soul and spirit are separate entities because God's Word can divide it.

What is the Bible and the Holy Spirit revealing to you right now regarding your innermost thoughts and desires? How does that impact your wellbeing?

> *So we do not lose heart. Though our outer self is wasting away, our inner self is being renewed day by day. For this light momentary affliction is preparing for us an eternal weight of glory beyond all comparison, as we look not to the things that are seen but to the things that are unseen. For the things that are seen are transient, but the things that are unseen are eternal.* (2 Corinthians 4:16–18 ESV)

According to these verses, how can we keep ourselves from not losing heart?

How do you deal with it when your soul is wounded?

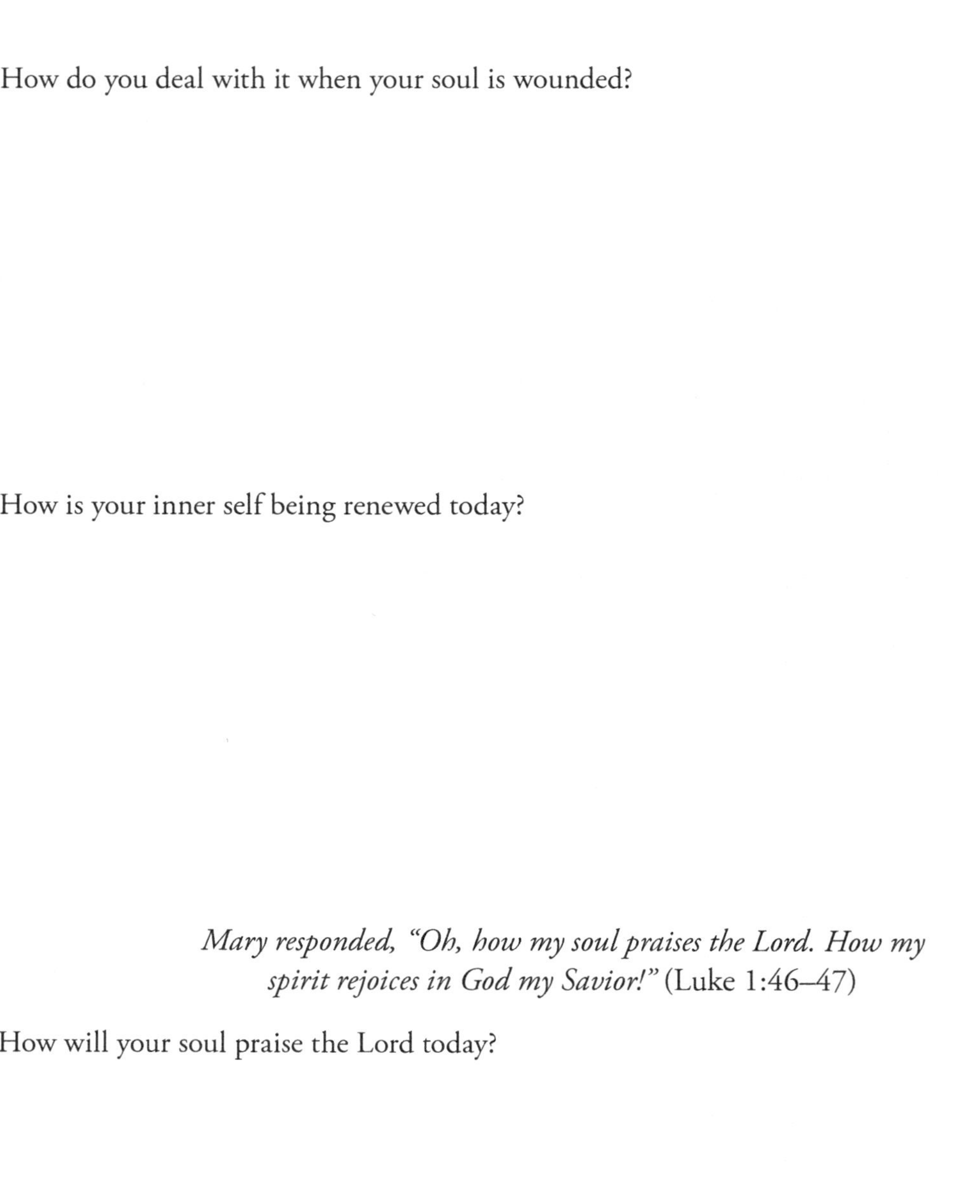

How is your inner self being renewed today?

Mary responded, "Oh, how my soul praises the Lord. How my spirit rejoices in God my Savior!" (Luke 1:46–47)

How will your soul praise the Lord today?

How will your spirit rejoice in God your Savior?

That according to the riches of his glory he may grant you to be strengthened with power through his Spirit in your inner being. (Ephesians 3:16 ESV)

From where does the power come to strengthen your inner being?

What weaknesses do you see with your soul and spirit?

How can you gain extra power and strength?

What are some spiritual practices you can learn to help you receive power from God?

> *Then Jesus said, "Come to me, all of you who are weary and carry heavy burdens, and I will give you rest. Take my yoke upon you. Let me teach you, because I am humble and gentle at heart, and you will find rest for your souls. For my yoke is easy to bear, and the burden I give you is light."* (Matthew 11:28–30)

What does this passage tell you about rest?

Why does your soul need rest? Where will you find it?

Why are you cast down, O my soul? And why are you disquieted within me? Hope in God; For I shall yet praise Him, The help of my countenance and my God. (Psalm 42:11 NKJV)

When your soul is discouraged, where will you find your hope?

How does praising God help your soul be encouraged?

"But the time is coming—indeed it's here now—when true worshipers will worship the Father in spirit and in truth. The Father is looking for those who will worship him that way. For God is Spirit, so those who worship him must worship in spirit and in truth." (John 4:23–24)

How do you worship God in spirit?

How do you worship God in truth?

Truly my soul silently waits for God; From Him comes my salvation.
(Psalm 62:1 NKJV)

Why does the soul specifically (it is singled out here) need to be saved? I wonder if it's because that is where our will resides. When we choose to sin, that is an act of the will. An act of the soul. Yes, that would need saving!

Extra reading:

- Psalm 63:1
- 1 Thessalonians 5:23–24
- 3 John 1:2
- 1 Corinthians 15:51–58
- Psalm 23:3
- Psalm 19:7
- Psalm 130:5
- Proverbs 16:24
- Romans 7:22
- Matthew 16:26
- Psalm 103:1

Help Me!

What do we do with this knowledge? The best way we can apply it is to know that our souls and spirits matter to God. He breathed into Adam, and he became a living soul. We worship God in spirit and in truth. So yes, our inner being is important to God. That doesn't mean our body does not serve a purpose—but we'll look at that later. For the sake of this chapter, let's focus our attention on inner being.

What do I need to detox or fast from to refresh my soul and spirit?

Let's look again at the definition of wellbeing: the state of being happy, comfortable, or healthy. It is a wellness that goes beyond physical health. A condition of contentment in soul and spirit.

Answer these questions:

- What is God making available to me so I have wellbeing of soul and spirit?

- What do I need to change or address for soul and spirit wellbeing?

- What is broken in my soul and spirit that needs healing?

- What are the distracters from my soul and spirit wellbeing?

- What can I do to refresh my soul and spirit?

- How can I find rest for my soul and spirit?

- How do I approach my pursuit of wellbeing for soul differently than I do for my spirit?

- What do I need to detox or fast from to refresh my soul and spirit?

In order to pursue wellbeing of soul and spirit, which do you need to do?

- Change your schedule
- Adjust your perspective
- Redirect your focus
- Infuse your spiritual growth
- Make a change in your environment
- Spark your passion with a new project
- Connect with a kindred spirit
- Say no more
- Say yes to something better
- Give yourself permission to relax

Homework

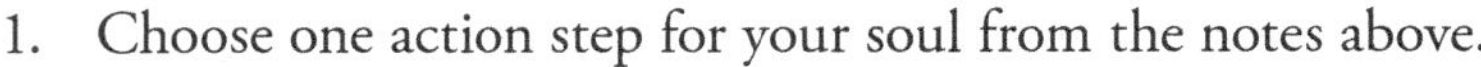

1. Choose one action step for your soul from the notes above.

2. Choose one action step for your spirit from the notes above.

3. Read the extra Bible verses for more knowledge on the topic.
4. What struggles have you had this week? List them and brainstorm ways to prevent or overcome them moving forward.

Health Check

Body: How is my body taking the brunt of my busy schedule? What needs to change?

Soul: Does my soul feel squelched? How can I release it to experience greater God-potential and allow my personality to shine more?

Spirit: When was the last time I truly communed with God, my spirit to his Spirit? What practices of personal faith can I learn or do more often so I worship him in spirit and in truth?

Hurrahs and Happy Dances

List your victories from the week and celebrate them. Share them with one of your cheerleaders. Note any aha! moments from this week.

Hope Quest

Father, I thank you for breathing life into me and not only forming my inner being but transforming it. I pray you will lead me on this journey toward wellbeing of my soul and spirit for your glory.

GRAB A PARTNER

I am empowered to do more when I get real with myself and also when I get real with an accountability partner or group. In this chapter, we'll take a look at how accountability equips us for much more than losing weight. When we reveal secret parts of ourselves to someone else, it's the closest thing we have to holding up a mirror and seeing our souls.

Think of accountability as having someone on your side. They offer support. They want what is best for you. Be sure to agree in advance how you want them to support you. Do you want their prodding, their empathy, their advice? They provide encouragement and wisdom.

Heartstrings

Turbulence and tons

The sounds of shouts and groans during our sudden drop weren't coming from a roller coaster ride but from a flight on a thirty-passenger prop plane. The ride was turbulent, and the seat belt sign was on most of the trip. We experienced many sudden drops and speeding nose dives. It made some sick and others pray. Being back on solid ground and breathing fresh air was never so sweet as when we landed from our bumpy ride.

My weight has also had a bumpy ride with similar rises and dips. To get back on track in the middle of this metamorphosis, I rejoined a weight-loss group. The accountability was just what I needed at the time. Having the weight come off is as liberating as being on solid ground after that turbulent flight.

When we reveal secret parts of ourselves to someone else, it's the closest thing we have to holding up a mirror and seeing our souls.

Both situations remind me we must get back to a firm foundation to find our constant source of strength. It takes the turbulence in our life journeys for us to appreciate the times of calm. We often pray more during the rocky times, but we are also tempted to focus on how bad we have it. We gain assurance from the fresh air of the Spirit and the reliability of the Word. One thing of note: the solid ground and the fresh air from God (and during that flight) were both there even when we were experiencing turbulence, but we lost focus of that fact!

If you're reading this book without needing to lose weight, this chapter is still for you.

Just as I need accountability to lose weight, I also need accountability with another Christian who is further down the road of life to help with my overall wellbeing. Accountability makes me responsible for my actions and attitudes. Getting rid of other kinds of weight in my life and getting back on solid ground are two ingredients necessary for Christian maturity and growth.

Heavenly Insights

Confess your sins to each other and pray for each other so that you may be healed. The earnest prayer of a righteous person has great power and produces wonderful results. (James 5:16)

How difficult is it to tell someone else your flaws, weaknesses, and even sins? Why?

What does this verse show about the benefits of accountability?

"But don't begin until you count the cost. For who would begin construction of a building without first calculating the cost to see if there is enough money to finish it? Otherwise, you might complete only the foundation before running out of money, and then everyone would laugh at you." (Luke 14:28–29)

Make a plan before you enter into an accountability partnership and agree to the plan so you are both on the same page.

How long of a commitment are you making to each other, and what does it involve?

Dear brothers and sisters, if another believer is overcome by some sin, you who are godly should gently and humbly help that person back onto the right path. And be careful not to fall into the same temptation yourself. Share each other's burdens, and in this way obey the law of Christ. (Galatians 6:1–2)

What is the mindset to assume when approaching your accountability partner regarding their actions and attitudes that indicate they are stumbling?

How do we share each other's burdens?

> *Let the message about Christ, in all its richness, fill your lives. Teach and counsel each other with all the wisdom he gives. Sing psalms and hymns and spiritual songs to God with thankful hearts.* (Colossians 3:16)

From this passage, what can we offer others that will sharpen them?

Find an accountability partner who has godly wisdom to share—someone who will teach and counsel you from a position of joy in Christ.

Extra reading:

- Ecclesiastes 4:9–12
- Proverbs 27:17
- 1 Thessalonians 5:11
- Hebrews 4:13–16

Help Me!

Plan for it

What struggles have you had with accountability prior to now? What did not work about a previous accountability arrangement (group or partner)?

What benefits do you gain from accountability?

How are you a valuable accountability partner for someone else? What do you bring to the table to encourage them?

How will you recruit your help?

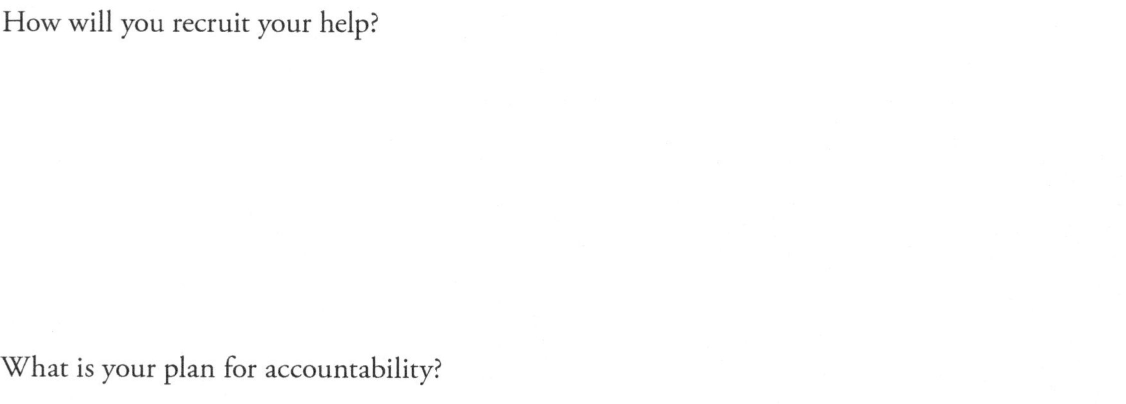

What is your plan for accountability?

Negative experience

My focus group told me they've had some less-than-favorable results with accountability partners in the past. They want a better method for picking and utilizing a new buddy for their wellbeing program. Some of their negative experiences include:

- They didn't follow through. They made a commitment and then slacked off.
- They gave excuses and just wanted to be placated rather than motivated toward better choices.
- They made me feel guilty when I had success and they did not.
- They were excessive in giving me advice they weren't personally living, yet not open to receiving suggestions.
- They made me feel uncomfortable. I can't think of someone with whom I'd feel safe revealing my shortcomings. It's a risk because of being burned before.

My partners

My accountability system helps me stay on track in every aspect of my life, including wellbeing. Over the years, I've gained motivation and support from a variety of sources, including these:

- **A fitness coach.** Sarah helped me brainstorm a workout plan that worked with my disabilities, goals, time, and equipment. I sent weekly updates for almost two years.
- **A wellbeing accountability partner.** Michelle and I emailed our goals and status reports weekly and still keep in touch with our updates.
- **Social media updates.** Sharing my journey online helped me stay real with the victories and struggles. It surrounded me with cheerleaders.

The triple-braided cord of accountability: honesty with God, a partner, and self.

- **Fitbit and My Fitness Pal.** This allowed me to monitor exercise and eating and to have a small social circle receive my updates. Sometimes their thumbs up fueled me for another day of being dedicated to the plan.
- **Classes.** I took Zumba at the gym and loved it! I also attended a diabetes education class. For several years, I led nutrition and exercise classes in our churches.
- **Weight-loss group.** When I needed added accountability facing the scale every week, I joined a national weight-loss group. I liked the online tools, the community of support, and the topics discussed by the leader.
- **Workout sessions with spouse.** Russ and I worked out at the gym together for about a year. This sparked extra motivation and improved our relationship at the same time. We also charted our progress. Our thirty-day smoothie challenge was a lot of fun.
- **Food prep with a buddy.** Sarah and I enjoyed doing bulk cooking together. Kathy and I met up via zoom for two cooking sessions.
- **Walking partners.** There are times I take a walk or hike with a friend. We go to a track, park, or simply walk in the neighborhood. We find a fast pace that works for both of us. When I can't be with someone in person, I often schedule a phone date and walk during that conversation. This even works for mall walking or walking fast at home!

- **Prayer partners.** Several of my friends provide valuable prayer support. One of my friends walked with me as we prayed aloud. It felt as if God was walking with us too. Prayer walking is powerful!

Pick your partner

- Select someone you feel safe with so you can be completely transparent. Offer the same accountability to them so it's a mutual partnership. Or make it a one-sided arrangement if they are already to goal but want to be there for you.
- Find one who understands your weaknesses yet encourages you to overcome them. Be bold with your partner so each of you pushes toward excellence yet also offers grace and mercy.

Get honest with accountability. Honest with God. Honest with your partner. Honest with self. These three become a triple-braided cord.

Homework

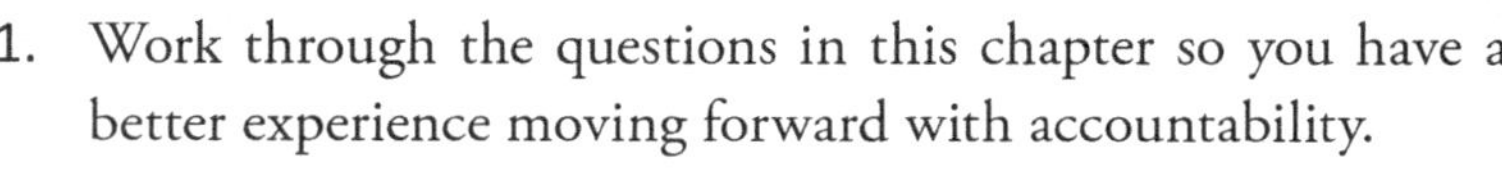

1. Work through the questions in this chapter so you have a better experience moving forward with accountability.
2. Recruit an accountability partner or plan to be active with a wellbeing group.
3. What struggles have you had this week? List them and brainstorm ways to prevent or overcome them moving forward.

Health Check

Body: Who would be a good exercise buddy or eating accountability partner for me?

Soul: Who in my life is my biggest uplifter?

Spirit: How will I be more accountable to God about my wellbeing choices?

Hurrahs and Happy Dances

List your victories from the week and celebrate them. Share them with one of your cheerleaders. Note any aha! moments from this week.

Hope Quest

Father, you know I've been burned before with this accountability thing. It's hard for me to confide in someone else about such personal matters. Help me know who offers a safe place for my heart and will propel me forward. Most of all, I make a commitment to come to you with my struggles and seek your direction for victory.

EXPOSING EXCUSES

It's time to face up to our excuses. Any time we don't address what is holding us back, we delay experiencing long-lasting victories. We might cringe when we admit our reasons for not making the best choices for our health. Usually, our excuses reveal some very human struggles and weaknesses. Thankfully, we have a God who shows himself strong through our weakness.

Heartstrings

Poster child for obstacles

I'm the poster child when it comes to having nutrition and fitness obstacles. Frequently, those who read about my weight-loss success say they wish they could achieve the same outcome, and then they offer up reasons (or are they excuses?) for why they can't do it. That's when I tell them I used to delay my wellbeing by stating those same excuses, and if I can overcome them, so can they.

I have several diseases that challenge optimal quality of life. I've had more than twenty surgeries that left me more impaired than repaired. Side effects and symptoms are hard to fight, let alone endure. And the fatigue makes it hard to be motivated to move more when all I want to do is move less. I'm not telling you about my medical issues to gain your pity. I want my story to assure you that I understand what it's like to have challenges outside of our control that make this quest for wellbeing difficult. But we'll learn in this chapter, difficult does not mean impossible.

Heavenly Insights

You will notice in the verses below that you are not alone in taking on what God wants you to take on. But these passages do not promise it will be easy. Anything worth having is worth doing, despite the difficulties along the way!

The lazy person claims, "There's a lion on the road! Yes, I'm sure there's a lion out there!" (Proverbs 26:13)

I always love reading this excuse in the Bible. Who says God doesn't have a sense of humor? (It would have been impossible for lions to be on the streets of a walled city.)

Look at your excuses in light of the concepts below, and you will come to determine they are simply imaginary lions in the road, keeping you from going through the door to freedom.

[Jeremiah says] *"O Sovereign* LORD*! You made the heavens and earth by your strong hand and powerful arm. Nothing is too hard for you!"* (Jeremiah 32:17)

[God says] *"I am the* LORD*, the God of all the peoples of the world. Is anything too hard for me?"* (Jeremiah 32:27)

Look at your excuse list. What makes those things hard for you?

What makes them too hard for God?

Make a list of the times God did the impossible in your life. Keep the list handy as a reminder of what he's capable of doing.

For I can do everything through Christ, who gives me strength. (Philippians 4:13)

Who is the strength giver in this passage and how have you experienced that power before?

If God is in it, is there anything you can't do? Or maybe we should look at it this way: there are things we can't do, but there is nothing Christ can't do.

Next time you're tempted to say something on your wellbeing plan is impossible, flip the script and say it is God-possible.

Don't be afraid, for I am with you. Don't be discouraged, for I am your God. I will strengthen you and help you. I will hold you up with my victorious right hand. (Isaiah 41:10)

How is it you can overcome fear? Discouragement?

God will strengthen you and help you. Part of his work equips you to overcome your obstacles. Why do you think he wants to help you get past the things that hold you back?

When you know he's holding you up with his dominant, victorious hand, how does this become the pep talk you need to overcome your excuses?

Help Me!

What's holding you back?

Moving forward often requires learning from the past to get past it. What are you allowing to hold you back from wellbeing? It's time to get real and identify your challenges. When I faced my excuses, I asked myself, "Why do I think these reasons somehow give me permission not to try?" (Do you know the difference between a reason and an excuse? An *excuse* is what others give for not trying. A *reason* is how we label our weak excuses to try to make them sound legit. When someone else has an excuse, it sounds so lame—but when we have the same one, it feels so reasonable! Hopefully you can read the snark in my words.)

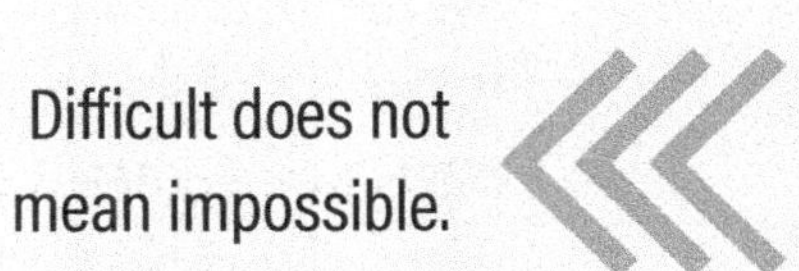

To overcome excuses, quit rationalizing and procrastinating. Identify and address the issues that keep you from eating and exercising for health. Here's a list of excuses from my friends and me:

- It isn't a good time—too much stress going on.
- My health conditions or medications caused the weight gain, so I might as well not try.
- I don't like to sweat.
- It's just too expensive.
- I'm too busy to take time for myself.

What is on your list?

Along the way, I realized I am in pursuit of more than physical wellbeing. I won't truly experience being well until I am whole in body, soul, and spirit. This is going to take a lifetime effort of *struggling*, *surviving*, and *succeeding* over and over again as God shapes me in his image. (And as the saying goes, "Rinse and repeat.")

Four ways I progressed despite obstacles

1. Mentally, I'm choosing wellbeing and giving up my excuses and reasons. Those excuses give me permission to not try, and I know I have to at least attempt health improvements despite the obstacles.
2. Wellbeing requires I invest time, energy, and focus. I've made the changes gradually to prevent setbacks. I adopted the role of physical trainer and nutritionist and still devoted the time necessary to customize a plan that works for me, even with my special challenges.
3. I have to be honest with myself when I have pain or other symptoms during or after workouts. I'm learning when the pain indicates I've exacerbated my health conditions. Sometimes pain doesn't mean I need to stop. It's merely my body growling at having to increase effort when it was dormant for a long time. Basic stirring-things-up pain might be the price for gaining overall wellness. I can put up with temporary soreness to get to my goal. (Muscles, tendons, ligaments, and bones are going to complain about us working them when they aren't used to it!) But I need to be wise and stop something or alter how I do it if I'm injuring myself or causing a setback in my health conditions. You'll recognize the difference as you go along. If possible, modify the exercise and continue, rather than quitting.
4. I cleared some time in my schedule to do this. Not just the workouts but the meal planning and preparation. I'm changing the way I do the rest of my daily functions. For example, I email shorter notes than my usual lengthy epistles to friends. I eat out less (food prep actually takes less time than going out to eat—it's healthier for me and gives me time I can spend exercising). I need to just plain old "show up."

God-control

This all started with the will to do it, and then I knew I could figure out a way. But it wasn't self-control. It was yielding all of that (the excuses and the "I do it myself" attitude) for God-control. I'm able to do things the physical therapists and surgeons said I'd never be able to do, so I know it's possible for you to figure out a way to face your excuses and customize a plan.

Be brave. That's why I'm calling you a Wellbeing Warrior. Be all in with this quest for your best. Don't let the obstacles become roadblocks or dead ends to your success. See them as merely speed bumps or detours. Even with challenges that hinder your progress—it's *still* progress.

At this point, my progress list is as long as my list of special challenges. Now, who wouldn't want that? Go for it!

This is a quest, not a quick fix.

Homework

1. Make your list of excuses for why you can't do this or how it is hard.

2. Make a reminder list of previous God-possible examples.

3. What struggles have you had this week? List them and brainstorm ways to prevent or overcome them moving forward.

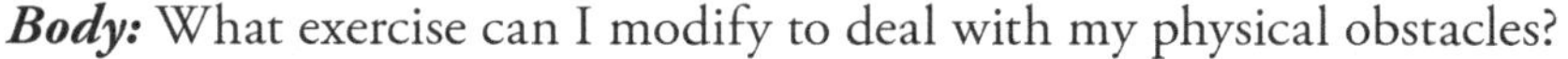

Health Check

Body: What exercise can I modify to deal with my physical obstacles?

Soul: What fear or discouragement does God want to help me overcome this week?

Spirit: How do I feel closer to God as I see him as my strength giver?

This is a quest, not a quick fix.

Hurrahs and Happy Dances

List your victories from the week and celebrate them. Share them with one of your cheerleaders. Note any aha! moments from this week.

Hope Quest

Lord, even now, this far into my quest for wellbeing, I'm allowing challenges to give me permission to not be all in. Give me back my zeal for conquering the reasons for failure and remind me when I cop out rather than cope. I'm addressing you as Lord because I want you to take control and lead the way.

HEALTH FOOD

Do you think your current food and lifestyle choices are helping you achieve and maintain health? If not, are you willing to make a change to benefit your health? One thing we often think of is "health food." But some people have aversions to it. Let's look at the term "health food" with our triple focus of body, soul, and spirit.

How do I make sure my *body* is healthy? What food does it take? What choices are necessary? What priorities will lead toward better physical health?

How do I make sure my *soul* is healthy? How can I make sure not to neglect it? What feeds my soul? You may have heard of *Chicken Soup for the Soul.* I'm sure there's an entire "grocery store" filled with items for our soul's pantry!

How do I make sure my *spirit* is healthy? What is on my spiritual foods menu? How can I best make this the number one emphasis in my life?

Heartstrings

I was told health is the absence of disease, but it has to be more than that, doesn't it? That sounds like how to survive, but I want to thrive! Then I heard health is a state of complete physical, mental, and social wellbeing and not merely the absence of disease or infirmity. I like that definition much better.

What does a healthy soul look like?

We have a pretty good idea of what health food looks like for the body. We know what it means to be physically healthy. But what does a healthy soul look like? I surveyed my Facebook friends, and they responded.

"In medicine, health is the absence of disease. So, to relate the same concept to the soul may make some think that it is the absence of pain or suffering. I think it is not that at all but the complete dependence on God for strength and passing those same blessings on to others." (Brenda Findley-Howe)

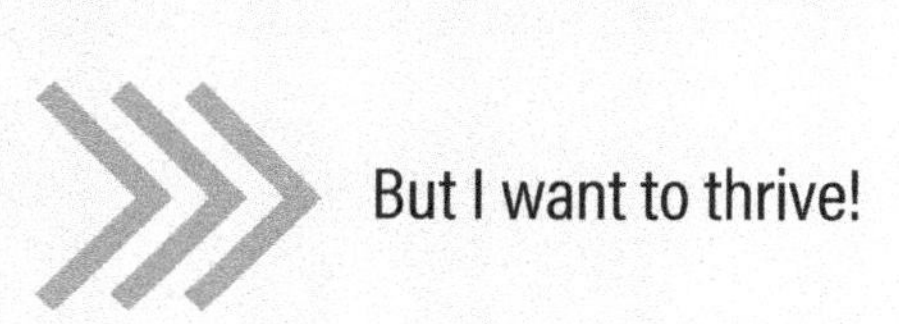

"A healthy soul is one that finds contentment. They are not constantly searching and longing for things they can't have or achieve. But they enjoy and cherish life as it is. It includes a satisfaction in God." (Carin LeRoy)

"A healthy soul is one that is quick to forgive and even quicker not to take offense in the first place. Is comfortable in her identity and doesn't compare herself to others. One that acknowledges where she came from and embraces the wonder of being alive. Naturally full of gratitude and grace. A healthy soul doesn't have to hide struggles or fear asking for help. One who soaks in the peace and healing that comes from being in God's presence." (Lisa-Anne Wooldridge)

"A healthy soul is one that can bounce back with joy, even after the deepest heartbreak." (Mindy Cantrell)

"Anything healthy is still growing. A healthy soul is one seeking growth." (Becki James)

"Not complaining and groaning. I'm sure that goes along with some of the others but you can always tell someone who's 'unhealthy' if they are always finding something to complain about. Lack of gratitude." (Melanie Reinke)

Heavenly Insights

So whether you eat or drink, or whatever you do, do it all for the glory of God.
(1 Corinthians 10:31)

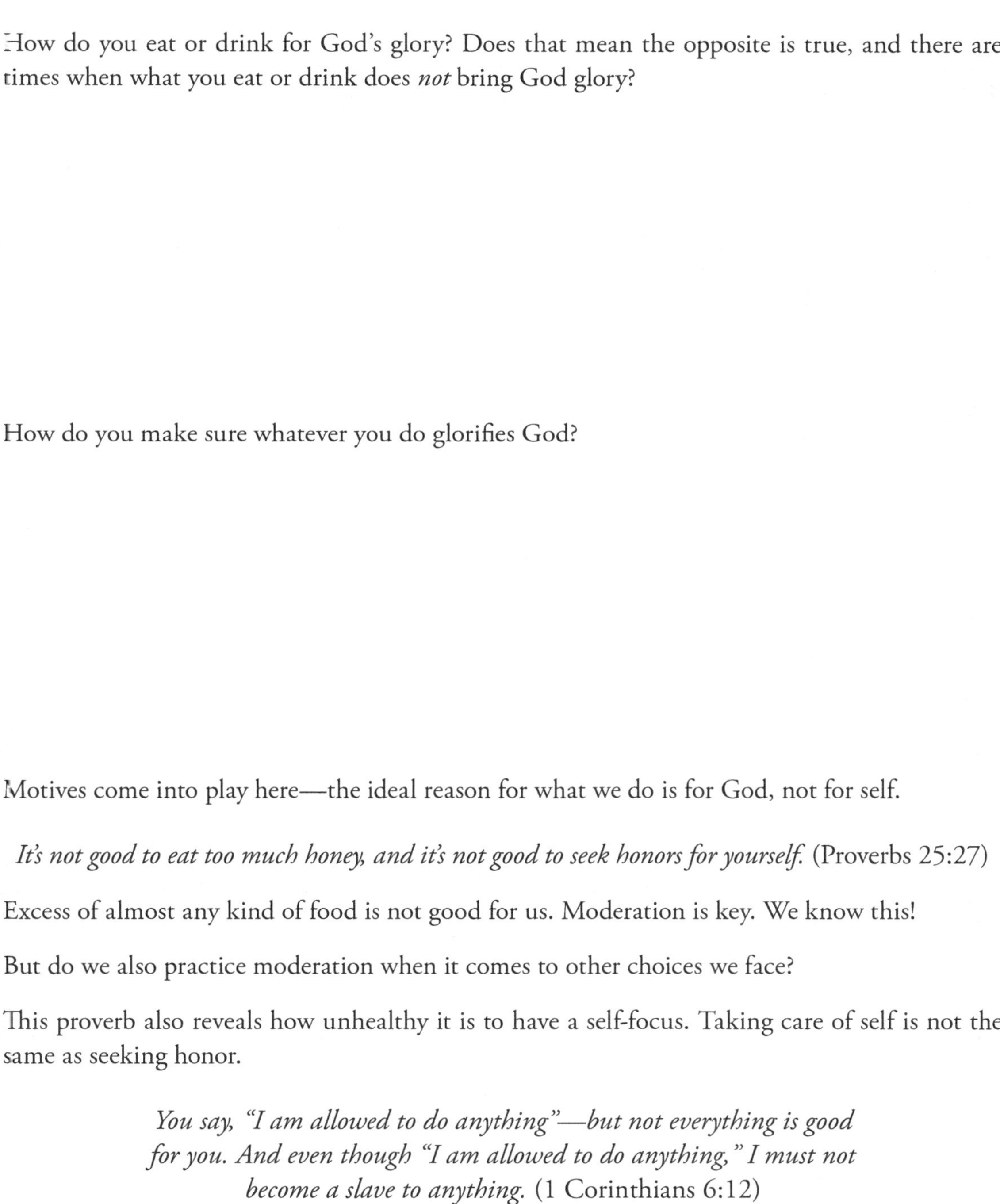

How do you eat or drink for God's glory? Does that mean the opposite is true, and there are times when what you eat or drink does *not* bring God glory?

How do you make sure whatever you do glorifies God?

Motives come into play here—the ideal reason for what we do is for God, not for self.

It's not good to eat too much honey, and it's not good to seek honors for yourself. (Proverbs 25:27)

Excess of almost any kind of food is not good for us. Moderation is key. We know this!

But do we also practice moderation when it comes to other choices we face?

This proverb also reveals how unhealthy it is to have a self-focus. Taking care of self is not the same as seeking honor.

You say, "I am allowed to do anything"—but not everything is good for you. And even though "I am allowed to do anything," I must not become a slave to anything. (1 Corinthians 6:12)

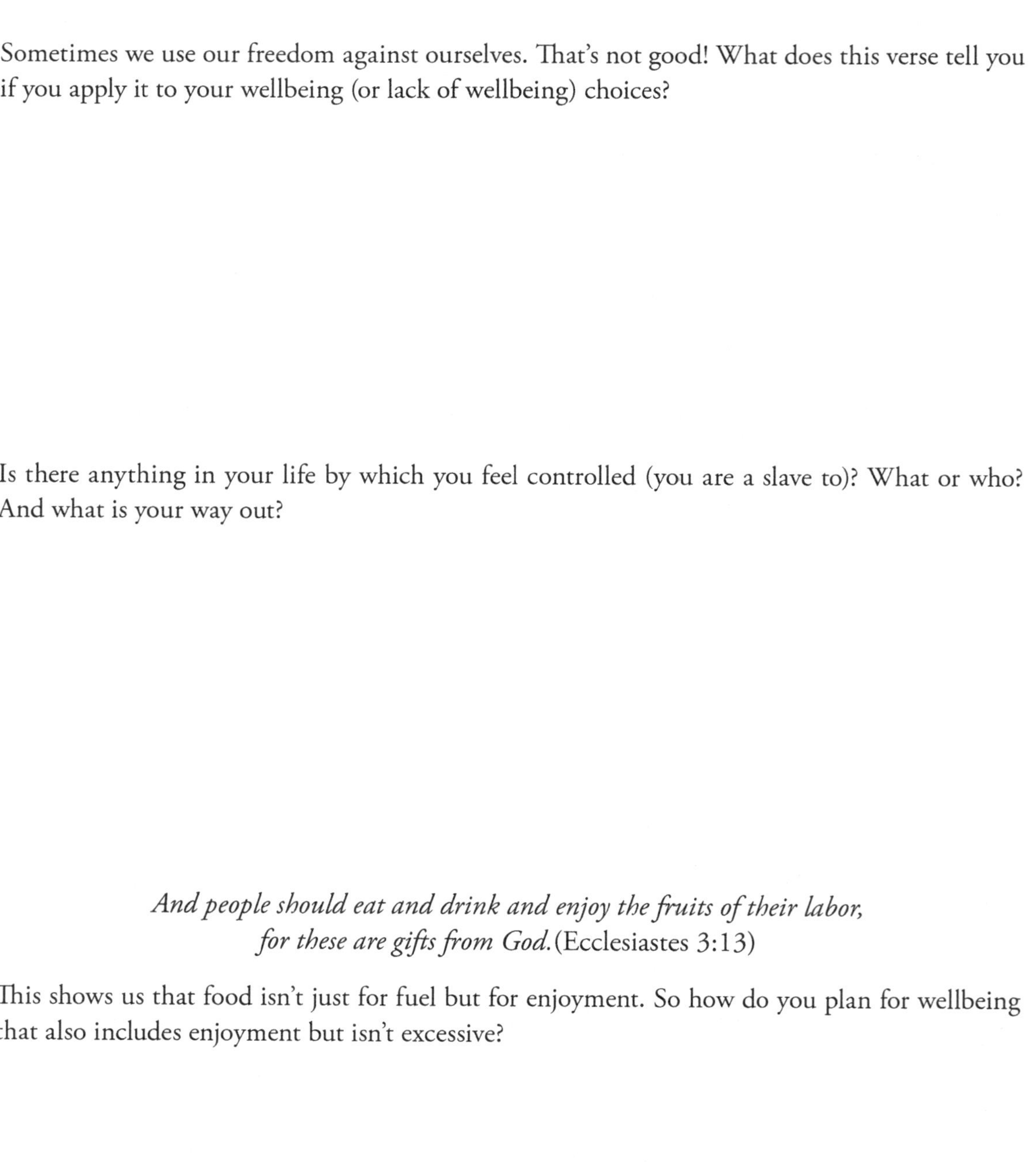

Sometimes we use our freedom against ourselves. That's not good! What does this verse tell you if you apply it to your wellbeing (or lack of wellbeing) choices?

Is there anything in your life by which you feel controlled (you are a slave to)? What or who? And what is your way out?

And people should eat and drink and enjoy the fruits of their labor, for these are gifts from God. (Ecclesiastes 3:13)

This shows us that food isn't just for fuel but for enjoyment. So how do you plan for wellbeing that also includes enjoyment but isn't excessive?

Are you a foodie? If so, think about what causes food to bring you enjoyment. Now think about food for the soul and spirit. How can you become a "foodie" in those realms as well?

"But don't be so concerned about perishable things like food. Spend your energy seeking the eternal life that the Son of Man can give you. For God the Father has given me the seal of his approval." (John 6:27)

Jesus replied, "I am the bread of life. Whoever comes to me will never be hungry again. Whoever believes in me will never be thirsty." (John 6:35)

We put so much emphasis on the provision of our physical needs despite those being temporary.

How does God want you to spend your energy?

What causes you to feel discontented when you have physical hunger or thirst and nothing seems to satisfy it? Describe hunger and thirst of the soul and spirit that has nothing to do with food and drink.

What is Jesus's remedy for that?

Help Me!

Tammy Anderud, part of the Wellbeing Warriors focus group, mentioned the goal of being a "heart-healthy person." You might think in a wellbeing group she meant a person who would pass the test at the cardiologist. No. She was referring to emotional health.

Let's continue to look at ways we can provide health food for body, soul, and spirit.

1. **Eat the rainbow.** How many types of produce do you have in your diet? Several times I've challenged myself to eat one hundred different types of produce in one hundred meals. It works perfectly in early summer when the farmers' markets are full of variety. Some of my friends joined the challenge but changed it to one hundred days instead of meals. Whatever you attempt, eating all the colors of the rainbow provides good nutrition. (Note: some have to limit certain types of produce due to food sensitivities or noticing they increase inflammation.) *Then God said, "Look! I have given you every seed-bearing plant throughout the earth and all the fruit trees for your food"* (Genesis 1:29).
2. **Detox where it really matters—the spirit.** Pursue holiness. *Because we have these promises, dear friends, let us cleanse ourselves from everything that can defile our body or spirit. And let us work toward complete holiness because we fear God* (2 Corinthians 7:1).
3. **Endure physical training.** I don't believe in "no pain, no gain," but I do know there are times I have to push myself toward the goal despite some soreness! *I discipline my body like an athlete, training it to do what it should. Otherwise, I fear that after preaching to others I myself might be disqualified* (1 Corinthians 9:27). This same principle can apply to spiritual training.

What are some other concepts that work to fuel us but not overload us?

1. **Moderation**. Show self-restraint when it comes to eating. Operate in control as you add in new lifestyle habits. (You don't need to tackle all of them at once.) Find balance in all things.
2. **Self-grace.** Sometimes it's hard to offer the benefit of grace to others (when we think they don't deserve it), but it's even more difficult to show ourselves grace. Treat yourself in the same manner God does. Forgive yourself for past mistakes and move forward without the weight of guilt consuming you.
3. **Quiet time.** We know that God's Word is the best food for the spirit. Having a timeout with God, focused on reading the Bible and praying, is good. Enhancing that quiet time to refuel both the soul and spirit is even better.

Homework

1. Take part in a food challenge similar to the one mentioned above.
2. Select some books to add to your "health food for the soul and spirit" library.
3. Read "Snack Time" and "Eating Healthy on a Budget" in the resource section.
4. What struggles have you had this week? List them and brainstorm ways to prevent or overcome them moving forward.

Health Check

Body: What food is on my healthy list?

Soul: What "food" do I need a steady diet of to help my inner being be healthy?

Spirit: What spiritual food will help me grow and mature?

Find balance in all things.

Hurrahs and Happy Dances

List your victories from the week and celebrate them. Share them with one of your cheerleaders. Note any aha! moments from this week.

Hope Quest

Father, you are my bread and water. May you provide health for my body, soul, and spirit, according to your plan for my life. Feed and fuel me with your spiritual health food to satisfy my needs.

ROADBLOCKS OR DETOURS

One of the reasons most people aren't able to stay on course with the goals God has given us for wellbeing and being well is because we face roadblocks or detours. Roadblocks stop our progress, and detours take us off the intended path for a short distance or amount of time. Our frustrations tempt us to give up. Instead, let's focus on a way to be committed to wellbeing for the long haul.

I admit to long time periods of plateaus and putting my best health choices on pause. Like others, I let up on being disciplined when my commitment wavers. But the foundational habits are still in place, and that is why I've been able to maintain a fifty-pound weight loss.

Heartstrings

Just having gone through the worst day of my year, I explained to someone that it felt as if I had fried my "motherboard." I needed a major reboot. The physical and emotional stress left a bruise on the wellbeing of my body, soul, and spirit. Sometimes when the charge icon for your life is down to 5 percent, all you can do is to shut off, just like my laptop does. So, as I write this, I'm listening to birds sing, watching a lizard change colors to adapt to his surroundings, and soaking up the sound of lake water lapping to the shoreline. The cool breeze is causing the tree limbs to wave and the leaves to rustle. If I let go of the stress and the to-do list, I realize life right at this moment is good. Sometimes, when we are hitting lots of roadblocks, we need to unplug and just be. Then we can recalibrate and recalculate—and all those other "re" words—to get back to it!

As I wrote my prayer team about my situation, I listed all that I felt I needed to do. And they helped me whittle away that long list into a bare minimum list I really had to do. The rest could wait. And I could rest in the wait. That was essential. If you are reading this at a time when you are hitting some kind of a wall, rest is essential for you too.

When we are too driven toward the world's definition of success, God gets our attention to refocus us. Sometimes he uses a roadblock to stop us in our tracks, so we turn toward his direction. Just ask Balaam, a man in the Bible who got the surprise of a lifetime when a donkey spoke to him (Numbers 22). It's more important to discover what God wants with our wellbeing than to read advice from a popular magazine. Let's see what his Word says.

Heavenly Insights

Show me the right path, O Lord; point out the road for me to follow.
Lead me by your truth and teach me, for you are the God who saves me.
All day long I put my hope in you. (Psalm 25:4–5)

Do you seek God's direction for your wellbeing priorities? When you hit a roadblock or detour, ask him to show you the road he wants you to follow.

What are some elements to following God's lead, according to these verses?

When you look at those aspects, which actions are on God to fulfill, and which actions are on us to do?

The rest can wait. And I can rest in the wait.

We use our powerful God-tools for smashing warped philosophies, tearing down barriers erected against the truth of God, fitting every loose thought and emotion and impulse into the structure of life shaped by Christ. Our tools are ready at hand for clearing the ground of every obstruction and building lives of obedience into maturity. (2 Corinthians 10:5–6 MSG)

I love how this paraphrase talks about having powerful God-tools ready at hand. What are the tools God gives us to deal with roadblocks and detours?

How does taking care of the difficult distractions of life help us mature?

This passage discusses building lives of obedience. What choices of yours stray from obeying God's principles and direction?

The author of *The Message* (Eugene H. Peterson), who wrote the paraphrase above, is also known for another title he wrote: *A Long Obedience in the Same Direction.* That says a lot, doesn't it?

> *We can rejoice, too, when we run into problems and trials, for we know that they help us develop endurance. And endurance develops strength of character, and character strengthens our confident hope of salvation. And this hope will not lead to disappointment. For we know how dearly God loves us, because he has given us the Holy Spirit to fill our hearts with his love.* (Romans 5:3–5)

How in the world can we rejoice when we are going through difficult circumstances?

How is your current trial helping you build endurance?

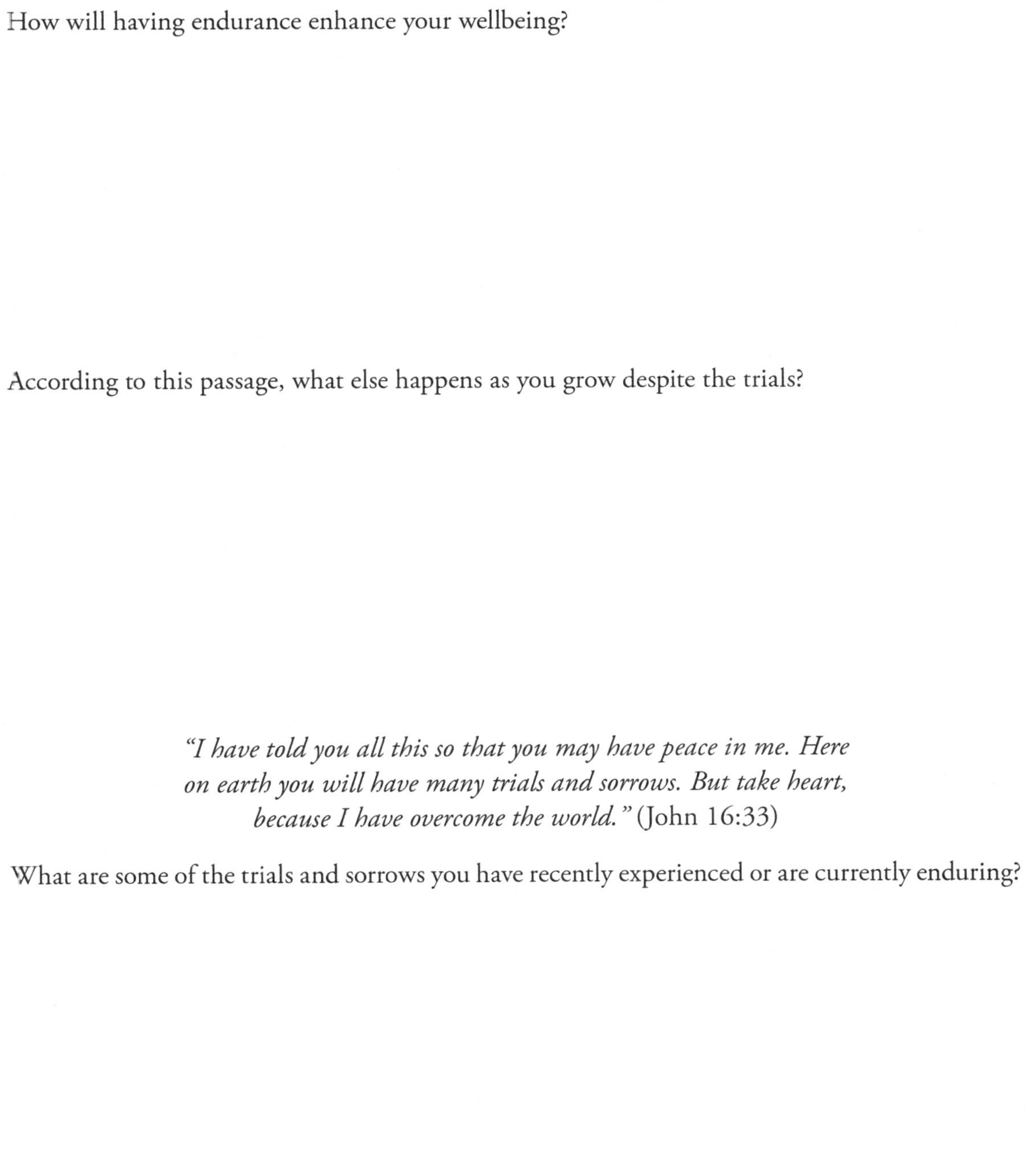

How will having endurance enhance your wellbeing?

According to this passage, what else happens as you grow despite the trials?

"I have told you all this so that you may have peace in me. Here on earth you will have many trials and sorrows. But take heart, because I have overcome the world." (John 16:33)

What are some of the trials and sorrows you have recently experienced or are currently enduring?

We can have peace in the Lord despite the issues that lead to the absence of peace. Why? Because we know that Jesus has overcome the world. In Jesus, we can overcome any roadblock or detour, in some way, as long as it aligns with his will.

Take some time to hear Jesus telling you to "take heart."

Help Me!

Face your issues

It's time to name your roadblocks and detours and decide how you're going to deal with them. When I polled my focus group, they listed several problems that exacerbate their struggles. Challenges such as these:

- Chronic health conditions
- Fatigue and pain
- Family issues
- Financial struggles
- Work stress
- Unsupportive loved ones
- Self-sabotage

Bare minimums for bad days

Just as my prayer team helped me develop a bare minimum list when I was having a particularly bad time of it, I encourage you to develop a *bad day plan*.

Answer these questions to help you get back on track:

- What does a bad day look like to you?

- On those worst days, do you feel as if you're supposed to self-motivate somehow and power through? Or do you think you need to give yourself grace to let up on not pushing so hard, even if it means altering your goals a bit?

- Is it time to add space and pace your activities to allow for mental and physical rest stops?

- What will you do when the mental and physical fatigue overwhelm you?

- What is your bare minimum list? It's so important not to neglect self-care during difficult times. (Read ahead to our self-care chapter if you need that right now.)

- What pain level indicates a no-exercise day for you?

Just one thing

Sometimes it's impossible to focus on achieving more than one action step for wellbeing on bad days. But it isn't just bad days that can do us in (if we let them). Sometimes a busy week will set us back just as much as a bad day. A busy week makes us feel as if we simply can't do one more thing. To prevent a sense of overwhelm (what I call the overs-of-whelming because I'm so over it), develop a *busy week plan*. I have a card system for when I know I can't handle a complicated wellbeing program. On those weeks, I pull out my stack of cards and draw just one card a day. I *can* handle "just one thing." What would you have in your deck? Some of mine include:

- Eat four servings of produce today.
- Take a fifteen-minute nature walk and capture beauty with your camera.
- Phone a friend (it isn't just for game shows!).
- Avoid white carbs today.
- Spend some time coloring.
- Pull out a freezer meal.
- Listen to a new worship song. Read the lyrics as the song plays.
- Dance away the stress.
- Treat yourself to in-season fruit and an ounce of cheese.
- Read a book for pleasure in place of thirty minutes online or TV time.

Homework

1. Make a list of your physical limitations. Decide what you need to do to work around them to get to a state of wellbeing. Create a plan.

2. Journal a prayer admitting your frustrations and fears regarding the detours and roadblocks to your wellbeing of body, soul, and spirit.

3. What struggles have you had this week? List them and brainstorm ways to prevent or overcome them moving forward.

Health Check

Body: What indicators do I need to heed so that I don't overdo it physically yet push myself enough to have improved fitness with less fatigue?

Soul: What will I do when I get discouraged by setbacks?

Spirit: How does God want me to define success?

Hurrahs and Happy Dances

List your victories from the week and celebrate them. Share them with one of your cheerleaders. Note any aha! moments from this week.

Hope Quest

Papa God, I fail most when I'm hit with roadblocks and detours. I want to give up rather than hunker down with a bare-necessities plan. Infuse me with the will to make good choices even on the toughest days.

NOT IN THE MOOD TO MOVE

Most people I know are divided into two camps: people who like to exercise (or at least like the benefits of it enough to do it) and those who despise it. Even people who like it (me!) sometimes don't feel like it. We either have a physical reason for not being up to exercising, we have time constraints, or our "want to" is missing. This chapter will discuss why we're not in the mood to move and how to squeeze in exercise anyway. It has to be a soul-move (choice of the inner being) before we feel like getting our bodies to move.

Heartstrings

I posted a survey on Facebook and asked my friends why they didn't want to exercise. I love the humor in some of the responses (it's fun to think of it from a playful perspective) and also appreciate their honesty.

Reasons for not exercising:

- I feel worse or too tired after exercise.
- I have an injury or bad back. Pain anywhere is a big deterrent.

- I don't like working out at a gym. Others look and talk to me in a condescending way. I don't like to work out in front of an audience. I tend to compare myself and come out on the losing end. I don't want to look/feel out of shape, and besides, it's too expensive.
- I use my home exercise equipment for hanging clothes.
- I hate to sweat.
- I don't have time. I get up early every morning, and most days after work, I'm done in. I'm just too busy.
- The treadmill is not my friend. Once I slipped on the treadmill belt, and now I don't trust it. I always walk too far from the console, and it pulls out the panic button. My sneakers squeak on the belt, and the sound bothers me.
- I keep getting interrupted by kids and pets.
- Exercise is boring.
- It's hard to eat and walk at the same time. I need both hands!
- I'm lazy.
- It's too hot/cold/dry/humid/windy/rainy/noisy/quiet!
- I already get enough steps in with regular life.
- I can't do the exercise I want to do (pool) because it's closed.
- I start a program, then when it gets interrupted, I don't ever get back to it.
- It would upset my longstanding and firmly established haphazard semi-routine.
- It keeps me from falling asleep at night.
- Exercise is against my religion!
- I don't know where to start.

Read through the reasons twice.

1. Do you identify with any of these reasons? Mark which ones sound like you.

2. What would you tell a friend if they said they knew they needed to exercise and then gave you these excuses? As you read through the list a second time, brainstorm for each point a work-around solution for someone to be active despite their reasons. You know . . . for your "friend."

It has to be a soul-move before we feel like getting our bodies to move.

Heavenly Insights

Physical training is good, but training for godliness is much better, promising benefits in this life and in the life to come. (1 Timothy 4:8)

In *The Message* paraphrase, it says: *Exercise daily in God—no spiritual flabbiness, please! Workouts in the gymnasium are useful, but a disciplined life in God is far more so, making you fit both today and forever.*

What kinds of training are good?

What are the benefits in this life? In the life to come?

What is your physical training of choice?

What is your training for godliness?

> *The faithful love of the LORD never ends! His mercies never cease. Great is his faithfulness; his mercies begin afresh each morning.* (Lamentations 3:22–23)

There are some things that never run out. Even though we run out of "want to" regarding exercise, what do we have endless supplies of, according to these verses?

Just as God's mercies begin afresh each morning, we get a chance for a do-over every day. If you went off your wellbeing plan, you can begin again. Give yourself the same faithful love and ceaseless mercy you receive from him.

> *The LORD directs the steps of the godly. He delights in every detail of their lives. Though they stumble, they will never fall, for the LORD holds them by the hand.* (Psalm 37:23–24)

If we seek to be godly, who do we look to for guidance?

How does God feel about dealing with our minuscule details?

What keeps us from falling?

> *No, dear brothers and sisters, I have not achieved it, but I focus on this one thing: Forgetting the past and looking forward to what lies ahead, I press on to reach the end of the race and receive the heavenly prize for which God, through Christ Jesus, is calling us.* (Philippians 3:13–14)

Even Paul, the writer of this passage, admitted being less than perfect. Learning from his example, what can we do when we aren't in the mood to exercise body, soul, and spirit?

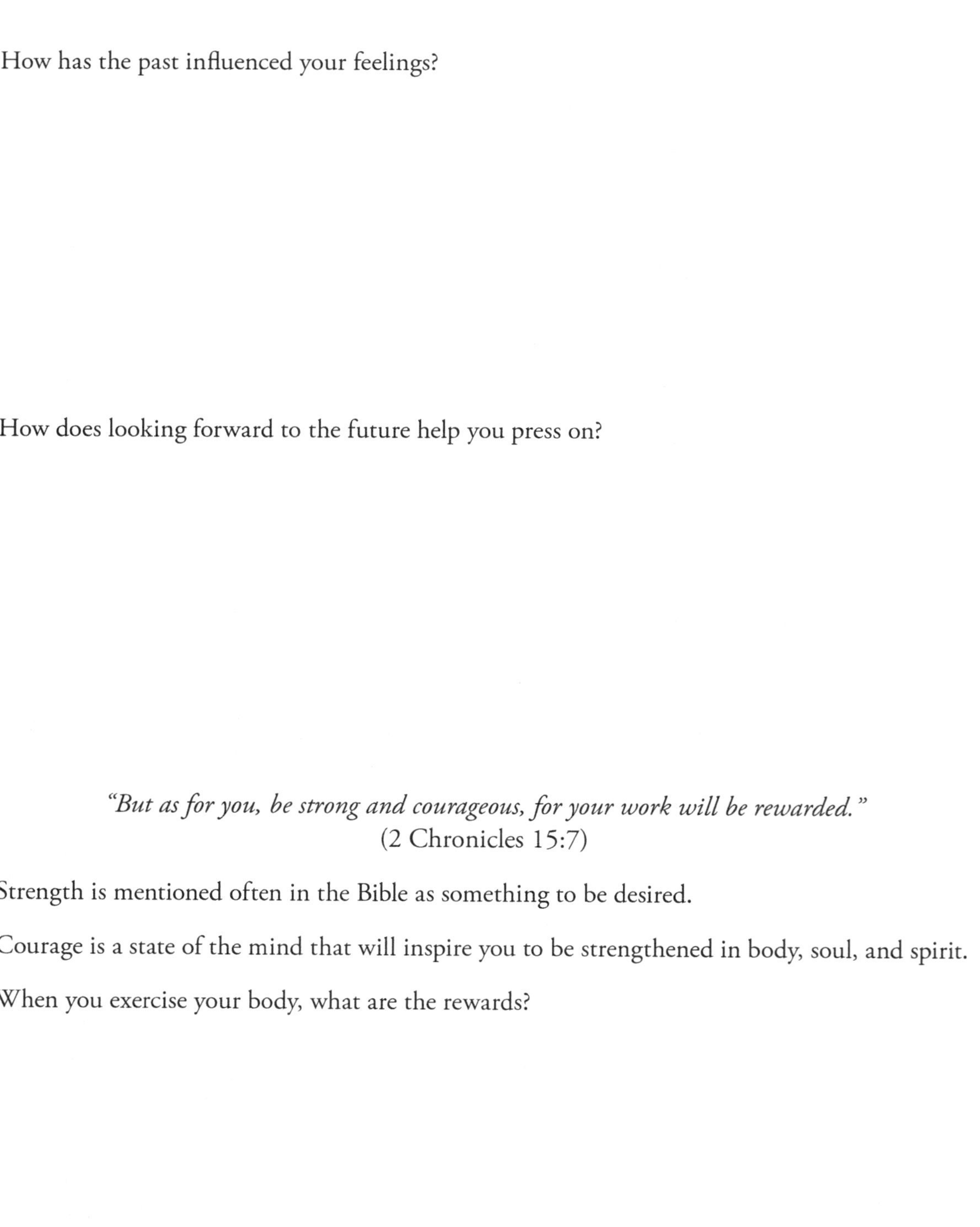

How has the past influenced your feelings?

How does looking forward to the future help you press on?

"But as for you, be strong and courageous, for your work will be rewarded."
(2 Chronicles 15:7)

Strength is mentioned often in the Bible as something to be desired.

Courage is a state of the mind that will inspire you to be strengthened in body, soul, and spirit.

When you exercise your body, what are the rewards?

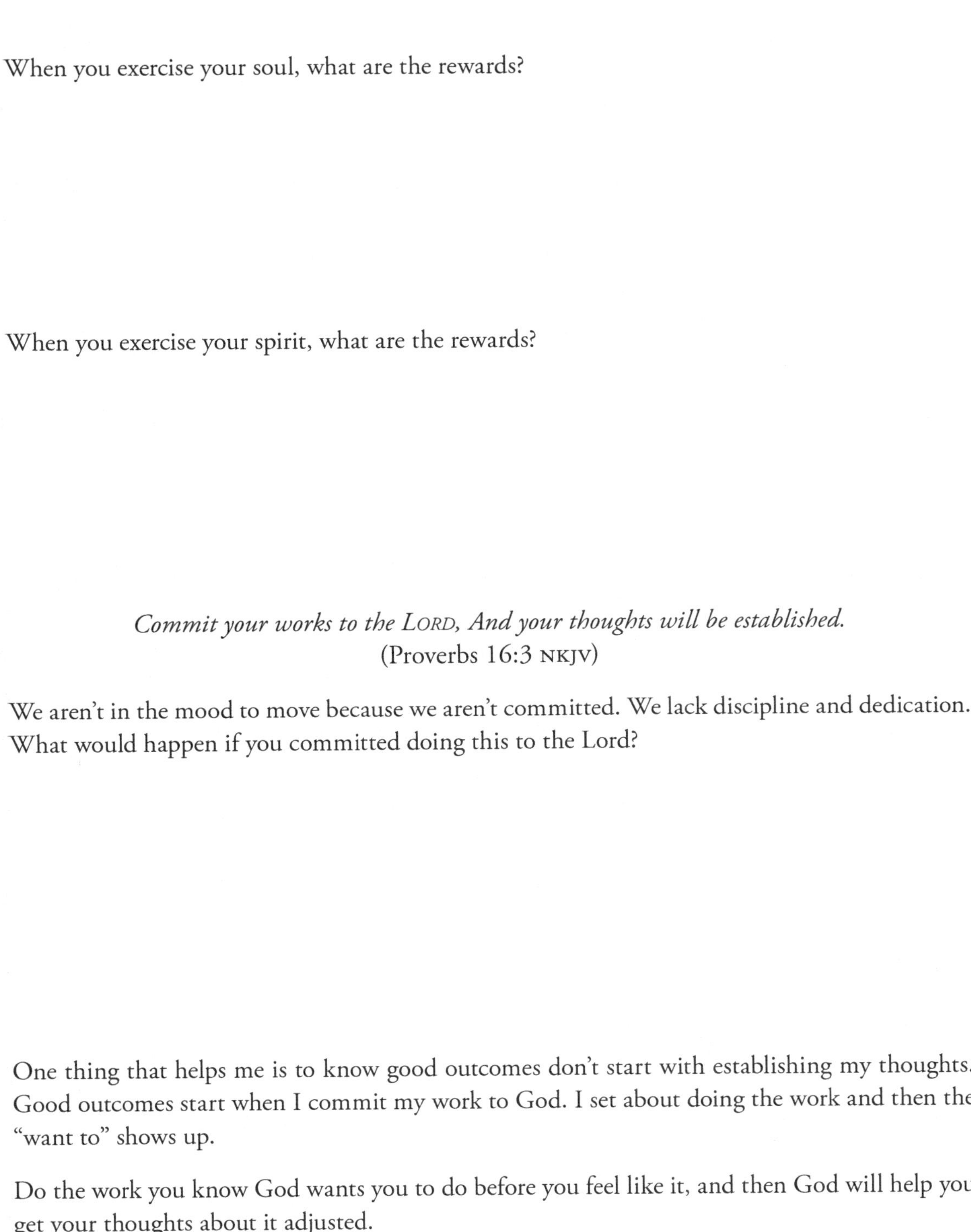

When you exercise your soul, what are the rewards?

When you exercise your spirit, what are the rewards?

Commit your works to the LORD, And your thoughts will be established.
(Proverbs 16:3 NKJV)

We aren't in the mood to move because we aren't committed. We lack discipline and dedication. What would happen if you committed doing this to the Lord?

One thing that helps me is to know good outcomes don't start with establishing my thoughts. Good outcomes start when I commit my work to God. I set about doing the work and then the "want to" shows up.

Do the work you know God wants you to do before you feel like it, and then God will help you get your thoughts about it adjusted.

Help Me

Points to remember:

- You don't have to exercise at a competition level for it to be good for you. Release the perfectionist pressure!
- Some exercise should be exhilarating, not exhausting.
- You can figure how to be active without breaking the bank or your schedule.
- It doesn't have to be every day to be beneficial. It also doesn't have to last an hour.
- Exercise is for whole health, not just the body.
- Many health insurance plans offer gym memberships or discounts (example: Silver Sneakers) and special programs based on your health needs.
- Exercise is therapy. Not only physical therapy but great for coping and for an emotional outlet.
- Some kind of exercise will suit you. Determine your exercise personality to get a good match with your exercise choice.
- Don't expect to feel good from exercise right away. It isn't about how you feel now but for the long haul.
- Do it anyway.

There are few days when you have a real reason not to exercise. You might need to reframe your definition of exercise. We definitely need to push ourselves when we're lazy or we've lost our dedication to healthy priorities. Decide on your deal-breakers for exercise. Your list might include:

- Fever or flare-up of disease or symptoms
- Death in the family
- Injury (although you can usually exercise a non-injured part)

Evaluate why you don't feel like exercising. Let's dig down deep and be honest with ourselves. Most reasons are just excuses because there is a solution if we really want to solve the problem.

There have been times I had to get creative with exercise, and I'm so glad I did.

- When my dad was dying in the hospital, I stayed there 24/7 for three weeks. When I wasn't by his side or sleeping, I needed the therapy of movement, so I took to the stairs. Climbing all those stairs did something that helped me, body, soul, and spirit.
- When I was deconditioned from a long-term illness and had a leg injury, I found an arm bike.
- When I couldn't afford a gym, I decided walking was my solution. I love to walk outdoors, but when the weather isn't agreeable, I walk indoors at a mall or in my home. (I probably have worn a walking path into the perimeter of my home!)
- When I am too busy to exercise, I schedule a work phone call and walk during it. I've expanded that plan to walking whenever I'm on the phone, whether for work or social calls.
- When staying at hotels, I like to use the gym equipment I don't have at home. There is rarely anyone in there, and I can even turn on the television or read an e-book while I exercise. Besides the hotel gym, most have a pool so you can try swimming, water walking, or water aerobics.

Homework

1. Make a list of all the reasons you don't feel like exercising. Then beside each reason, list a work-around solution.

2. Read "Strength Training" and "Back to the Gym" in the resource section.
3. Journal a prayer committing your work to God.

4. What struggles have you had this week? List them and brainstorm ways to prevent or overcome them moving forward.

Health Check

Body: What new type of exercise will I try this week?

Soul: What will I do to exercise my heart and mind this week?

Spirit: What exercise will draw me closer to the heart of God?

Set about doing the work before you feel like it, and then the "want to" will show up.

Hurrahs and Happy Dances

List your victories from the week and celebrate them. Share them with one of your cheerleaders. Note any aha! moments from this week.

Hope Quest

O God, my Life Coach, I need your motivation to help me live a disciplined life. My desire is to be fit inside and out, not just for today but for eternity.

A TIME TO REST

Rest is essential to wellbeing of body, soul, and spirit. Yet we all agree that rest is one of the most elusive elements discussed in this book. (It's so important, we have several chapters devoted to the topic!) Every person I talk to says they struggle with rest because of their busy schedules and stress-filled lives. Yet, I've learned I can be more productive in my doing hours when I make sure I have enough resting hours. (And conversely, if I don't rest, I am less productive in the same number of hours.) In this chapter, we'll discuss what rest means to us, what causes us to not feel rested, and what we can do to add more rest to our lives.

Often if we do the opposite of what causes us to feel unrested, we can add more rest to our week.

Heartstrings

As I write this, I am in a restful state of heart and mind. My soul has ceased striving. How? I'm borrowing a friend's place to do laundry. That might seem the opposite of rest, so let me explain. My life has been jam-packed with too much to do, too much drama and stress. My own home is not set up due to just moving and not having our storage containers delivered yet.

Do you know that cartoon clip where the kid says Mom, Mom, Muh-mom, Mommy . . . over and over? Can you relate? I might not have kids, but that is my life. I endure the pressing stress of my mom, husband, and dog all needing me.

Contrast that to my friend's house. She is away for the day. There is peace and quiet. She had the house tidied up and decorated for the season. A fragrant scent greeted me at the door. I perched my tired body on her comfy chair instead of the hard thrift-store kitchen chair at my still-barren home. She gave me her Wi-Fi code. I brought a coupon to save on my drive-thru lunch. I wonder if I could barter something with her just to have this wonderful retreat every so often.

When I surveyed Facebook friends asking them to tell me what rest means to them, they replied:

- Being able to do my own thing, at my own pace, with no interruptions.
- Turning off all the obligations and stresses in my head.
- Being at complete peace.
- Having no worries or stress.
- Pausing for idle body, mind, and spirit.
- Getting away, escaping from responsibilities.
- Relaxing, with a sense of safety and calm combined.
- Obtaining quality and quantity sleep.
- Doing fun things that bring me joy.
- Slowing down.

Rest requires faith, and a lack of soul rest is caused by fear and doubt. The Greek definition for "rest" means to cease, to be refreshed, and to abide.[2]

Restlessness is a symptom of being homesick for God's love. Because that's when true rest comes—when we can hunker down in his love and know it's enough—we don't have to perform or strive for perfection. Just be.

Heavenly Insights

The LORD is my shepherd; I shall not want. He makes me lie down in green pastures. He leads me beside still waters. He restores my soul. He leads me in paths of righteousness for his name's sake. Even though I walk through the valley of the shadow of death, I will fear no evil, for you are with me; your rod and your staff, they comfort me. You prepare a table before me in the presence of my enemies; you anoint my head with oil; my cup overflows. Surely goodness and mercy shall follow me all the days of my life, and I shall dwell in the house of the LORD forever. (Psalm 23:1–6 ESV)

Psalm 23 starts by assuring us the Lord takes care of our needs. Right after that, it shows how he makes us rest. Sort of like when Mom took care of me as a child by insisting I napped even when I didn't want to be still. Where does this psalm say God sends us? Green pastures and still waters—exactly what a sheep needs.

When I lie down and follow God's lead, he restores my soul. My soul is the invisible part of me that makes me who I am: my mind, emotions, and will.

To be restored means: re-establish, repair, rebuild. It's like giving my inner being mouth-to-mouth resuscitation! Could it be we have restoration only when we rest? If so, I'd better give it more importance in my life. It's what I need right now—how about you?

If we do the opposite of what causes us to feel unrested, we can add more rest to our week.

The remainder of the psalm shows other ways God puts our hearts and minds at ease. If you have some time today, take a look at Psalm 23 with that in mind.

> *Don't worry about anything; instead, pray about everything. Tell God what you need and thank him for all he has done. Then you will experience God's peace, which exceeds anything we can understand. His peace will guard your hearts and minds as you live in Christ Jesus.* (Philippians 4:6–7)

Think about your worries and concerns. The apostle Paul says here we aren't supposed to worry about anything. Can you find a concern on your worry list exempt from this?

What alternative does Paul give for worrying?

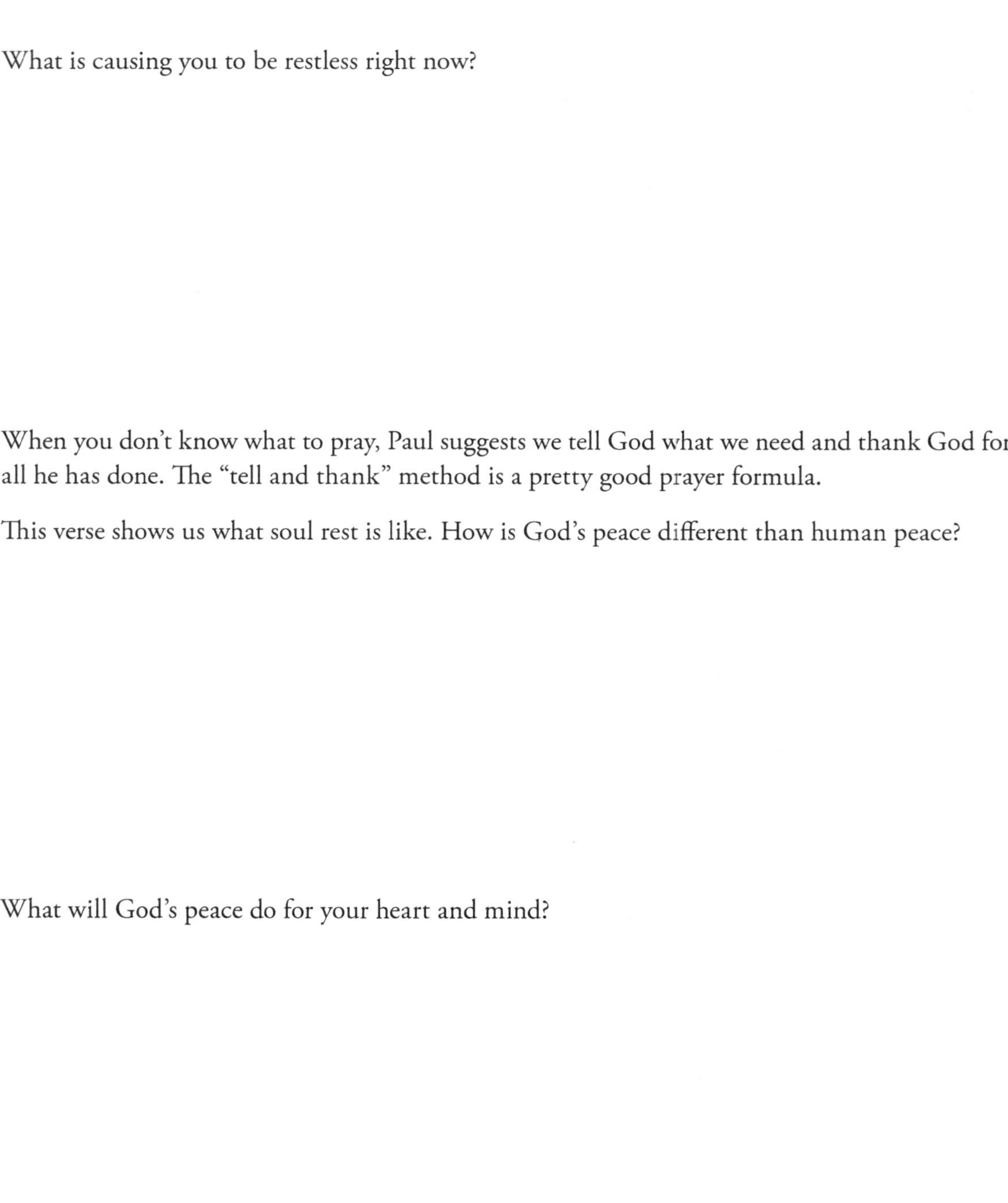

What is causing you to be restless right now?

When you don't know what to pray, Paul suggests we tell God what we need and thank God for all he has done. The "tell and thank" method is a pretty good prayer formula.

This verse shows us what soul rest is like. How is God's peace different than human peace?

What will God's peace do for your heart and mind?

Help Me!

It takes submission and surrender to settle down into God's rest. Instead, many of us go through life feeling restless. When we don't allow our hearts to be still, our emotions stay stirred up. We struggle with an unresolved issue. Unforgiveness. Bitterness. Hurt. Insecurity.

My Facebook friends agree. They listed what interferes with rest:

- Family, deadlines, responsibilities, demands, stress.
- Noise. Drama. Chaos.
- Not feeling safe.
- My upbringing—it was slovenly to rest or not be productive.
- Feeling guilty that I have things left to do.
- My mind. I imagine what could happen, begin to worry, and forget to trust God. Rewind and repeat.
- Anxiety and worry.
- Being overwhelmed by my own overzealous commitments.

It's wise to build your day of rest on a good foundation. Create your own list of what causes you to feel unrested. Then go back through that list and decide what you need to do to prevent those things from happening. Almost always, it goes back to having good boundaries, advocating for yourself, and saying no more. In another chapter, we'll discuss the *busy syndrome* and how to add more margin into your schedule.

Is there a mindset you need to retrain, reframe, and rescript?

The old script:

1. I'm being lazy if I rest.
2. I'm being selfish if I say no when someone needs me.
3. I'll never get to my goals if I stop to rest.
4. I have to be in control of my life to prevent being hurt or disappointed.
5. It's better to burn out than to rust out. (Some of my focus group had never heard this one. Several pastors taught me it's more desirable to work so hard you burn out than to do nothing and rust out from non-activity like an abandoned vehicle. That goes against a biblical foundation for rest.)

Counter each of those old statements with the matching number in the new script:

1. I will only have enough strength for tomorrow if I rest today.
2. I will be better equipped to help a few if I say no to the others to rest.
3. I will only get to my goals if I have enough energy to finish them.
4. When I yield control to God (it's his anyway), I can trust in him and rest.
5. It's better to have enough white-space margin to be refreshed so I can refresh others.

While you work to reveal your incorrect self-talk regarding rest, practice the presence of the Lord. Imagine God right by your side, as if you're both sitting on a park bench, visiting. Soak up any wisdom he shares with you regarding your lack of rest and need for rest. With God by your side, you will have the best balance between energy to do what needs to be done and resting. The energy he gives supplies what you need, not just physically but mentally.

Restlessness is a symptom of being homesick for God's love.

Homework

1. Make a list of what causes you to feel unrested, and beside each cause, list a remedy.

2. Practice the script flip idea. (Make self-talk cards or phone notes if necessary.)
3. Read "To Sleep, Divine!" in the resource section.
4. What struggles have you had this week? List them and brainstorm ways to prevent or overcome them moving forward.

Health Check

Body: What is one way I can add physical rest to my schedule?

Soul: What new mindset do I need to adopt?

Spirit: What Bible verse will help me make rest a priority?

Hurrahs and Happy Dances

List your victories from the week and celebrate them. Share them with one of your cheerleaders. Note any aha! moments from this week.

Hope Quest

Father:

Give rest to my **soul**. I relinquish control and trust in you.

Give rest to my **spirit**. I relinquish being too busy
and will connect with you in prayer.

Give rest to my **body**. I relinquish my worries and wonderings
and will meditate on your Word as I drift to sweet sleep.

COMPARISON TRAPS AND COMPETITIVE SPIRITS

As you've been on this Wellbeing Warrior journey for a while, you may have noticed some problems surfacing. Two of the common ones are comparison traps and competitive spirits. If you are doing well toward your goals, others will notice. Some of them will be jealous. Or perhaps you have watched others move closer to success while your own journey is taking longer. We can do a lot of damage when we allow our minds and hearts to be invested in comparison traps or if we develop a competitive spirit. (Or suffer when someone else responds that way to us because we're making positive changes.) How can you conquer these issues and crucify those pesky comparison traps and competitive spirits that stir up within you?

Heartstrings

Sometimes the worst comparison trap we get stuck in is when we compare ourselves with a former version of ourselves. A better version. A younger version. A fitter version. A thinner version. A stronger version.

I lifted weights at professional levels and was preparing to compete when I was afflicted with a life-altering disease at age twenty-eight. Since then, I almost died a couple of times, and have been in a wheelchair a lot. I always rehab and always do what I can to return to physical fitness. But I want to confess a battle that happens in my head sometimes.

When I'm in "the trap," I compare what I can do now to what I could do in my prime. And I grieved that I started losing fitness before I ever really hit my prime due to my age when I was afflicted. Here's the thing—even people who *don't* have ongoing medical issues can't stay at their prime game forever. I remind myself of that fact. I can either be a couch potato, or I can live life at 100 percent—even if my 100 percent today is less than my 100 percent when I was at my prime conditioning.

Deconditioning isn't merely stalling out in neutral—it's actually sliding backward. Doing what I can prevents the deconditioning that happens from settling for less than today's best. I've had to modify what I do. I've found other activities that give me that same adrenalin rush as lifting heavy weights. It's like anything else in life: I may not be able to do *everything*, but I'm able to do *something*.

When our health causes us to lose something we love, there is a grief involved that is as bad as having someone die. If you are dealing with that, give yourself some extra grace. I'm sure others do. Gracing your grief is different than pity. It's simply being real that our current circumstances are different than before. It's hard having to say goodbye to the glory of our former ability. But we know all of this is temporary compared to eternity.

> *[But what of that?] For I consider that the sufferings of this present time (this present life) are not worth being compared with the glory that is about to be revealed to us and in us and for us and conferred on us!* (Romans 8:18 AMPC)

Heavenly Insights

> *Obviously, I'm not trying to win the approval of people, but of God. If pleasing people were my goal, I would not be Christ's servant.* (Galatians 1:10)

Is one cause of comparison traps and competitive spirits the fact that you are worried about what others think of you? How do you address this in your life?

It's easy to say that our desire is to have God's approval and we want to please God by being Christ's servant. But it's harder to put into practice. What are some of your struggles with this?

> *So here's what I want you to do, God helping you: Take your everyday, ordinary life—your sleeping, eating, going-to-work, and walking-around life—and place it before God as an offering. Embracing what God does for you is the best thing you can do for him. Don't become so well-adjusted to your culture that you fit into it without even thinking. Instead, fix your attention on God. You'll be changed from the inside out. Readily recognize what he wants from you, and quickly respond to it. Unlike the culture around you, always dragging you down to its level of immaturity, God brings the best out of you, develops well-formed maturity in you. I'm speaking to you out of deep gratitude for all that God has given me, and especially as I have responsibilities in relation to you. Living then, as every one of you does, in pure grace, it's important that you not misinterpret yourselves as people who are bringing this goodness to God. No, God brings it all to you. The only accurate way to understand ourselves is by what God is and by what he does for us, not by what we are and what we do for him.* (Romans 12:1–3 MSG)

What does it take to give your body to God?

What is the motivating factor?

We know this is not a one-and-done act of surrender, so when is it necessary to present your body to God again?

Another version talks about being a living and holy sacrifice. What does that look like?

Sometimes the worst comparison trap we get stuck in is when we compare ourselves with a former version of ourselves.

Do you fight with the idea that God can find your sacrifice acceptable? Write about your struggle.

How do you worship God with your living sacrifice?

What happens when we copy the behavior and attitudes of the culture around us?

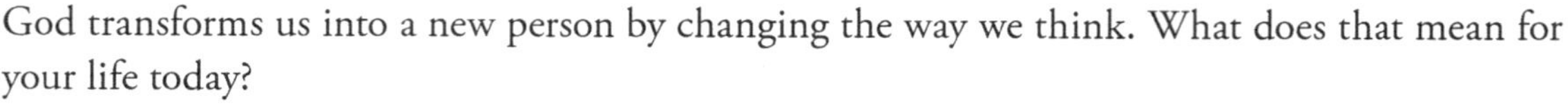

God transforms us into a new person by changing the way we think. What does that mean for your life today?

What do you sense is God's will for you regarding wellbeing of body, soul, and spirit?

Extra reading:

- Proverbs 13:10
- Psalm 139:14
- Galatians 6:3–5
- 1 Timothy 6:6–8
- Luke 18:9–14

Help Me!

What is your biggest struggle with comparison traps? Do you fall prey to any of these? Circle the ones to which you relate.

- I wish I had a tiny waist like Tina.
- Why can't I be as successful as Mandy?

- I can't believe Belinda said that. I would never say such a thing!
- I don't understand how Teresa can have so much faith despite all the trials she's gone through. I can't seem to muster up even a mustard-seed-sized faith!
- I'm jealous of all the attention Denise is getting at work. I did the heavy lifting on that project, and she's getting all the glory!
- Maggie is losing three times the pounds in half the time as me, and we're on the same program. Why can't I lose more weight?
- If I didn't have all these terrible circumstances, I could get ahead like Cindy. She doesn't have my [fill in the blank] to deal with!

Steps to comparison-trap freedom

1. **Catch yourself in the trap, call yourself on it, and cancel the thought.** Read 2 Corinthians 10:3–4, 12. In the passage, it's discussing Paul's credentials and the rumors about him from false teachers. We can learn from his method of resisting comparison traps. What are some of the lies your reasoning tells you about your wellbeing progress (or lack of progress)?

   How do you counter this temptation to compare yourself with others or compare with a younger version of yourself?

2. **Keep your eyes on your own work.** If life is a test, are you looking for answers on another person's paper, or do you focus on your own progress? We are only responsible for our own results. Read Galatians 6:4–5.
3. **Take an honest evaluation of yourself, using the measuring stick of faith.** Read Romans 12:3. The NLT version ends with, *Be honest in your evaluation of yourselves, measuring yourselves by the faith God has given us.* What does that look like to you? If you aren't sure, take some time to research this passage and read biblical articles on the subject.
4. **Have an impress-others-ectomy.** Let go of your self-focus. Then you are able to view others as better than yourself without it hurting your heart or making you feel less than. This mindset shift allows you to serve them without getting resentful. Who do you find yourself trying to impress? Why? How can you change that?

Competitive spirit—spitfires or spits fire?

When I researched the term *competitive spirit* online, I found that nine out of ten articles view this as a positive attribute. That's quite revealing, isn't it? They viewed this as a necessary trait to being successful.

What are the dangers of having a competitive spirit?

When left unchecked, do you tend to have a low self-esteem or a magnified self-esteem?

How can you trade this for a biblical view of yourself?

What examples in your life point to being competitive in a way that is dangerous to your mind-set, or even sinful?

Is it possible to have a healthy competitive spirit that motivates self-improvement without trying to be better than others? If so, how can you tap into that kind of competition?

Homework

1. Spend time going deeper with your thoughts and answers in the above sections. Journal this in the allowed space.
2. Report in with your accountability partner and discuss what you're learning about yourself. Give her specific ways to pray for you. (Or report this to your group if you want more support.)
3. What struggles have you had this week? List them and brainstorm ways to prevent or overcome them moving forward.

Health Check

Body: How do I view my body image? What adjustments do I need to make?

Soul: What part of my inner being do I put down and belittle? I wouldn't say those words to anyone else.

Spirit: Do I put undue pressure on myself about my relationship with God? It isn't about performance.

If life is a test, are you looking for answers on another person's paper or do you focus on your own progress?

Hurrahs and Happy Dances

List your victories from the week and celebrate them. Share them with one of your cheerleaders. Note any aha! moments from this week.

Hope Quest

O Father, I need your help. I struggle with comparison traps. Help me catch and release them. May I crucify my competitive spirit and replace it with a biblical view of myself and others.

SELF-CARE ISN'T SELFISH

I've read several articles that say self-care is selfish because it indulges personal satisfaction rather than investing in God and others. They say it's poor stewardship of money and time. While I do know some who engage in selfish-care instead of godly self-care, only the person choosing self-care and soul-care can determine if their motives are pure.

What are warning signs of being self-absorbed? One is when the individual frequently puts themselves first and is unable to see the needs of others. They sacrifice the family budget for personal treats (and sometimes, these become addictions). Obviously, any time we neglect what is important for temporary satisfaction, we take self-care in the wrong direction.

But, if utilizing self-care/soul-care is for the purpose of taking care of yourself, you will end up with more of *you* to serve God and minister to others.

Heartstrings

If you've faced an acute or chronic medical diagnosis, you know how difficult it can be to find your optimal best. My best might be someone else's 65 percent! No matter our health status, we all struggle with true wellness. In my pursuit of wellbeing and being well, I keep finding I have so much to learn. More than that, I need to make it a priority to implement what I've already learned.

I remind myself that I'm a three-part being. Body, soul, and spirit. Even though we won't take our bodies to heaven with us, it's still important to take care of the temple. It's the only one we get while we live in our temporary home. Good care of body, soul, and spirit is a mindful application of biblical concepts.

Being selfish means the only person you are concerned about is yourself. You are self-absorbed, wanting to please your own desires at the neglect of what others need. In contrast, self-care means taking personal responsibility for the one *you* God has put on earth so you can fulfill his purpose in you.

Often, we neglect ourselves, thinking it's part of the J.O.Y. pattern to focus first on *Jesus*, then on *Others*, and put *You* last. And yes, the Bible does address the importance of having a selfless mindset. But it isn't selfish to take care of yourself. One person made a joke that said the J.O.Y. pattern is actually Jesus, Ourselves, and Y'all. My guess is, God wants us to take care of all those elements. Part of self-love is self-care. We just have to figure out a way to do it that puts the glory back on God, rather than becoming fixated on self.

Heavenly Insights

Jesus said, "The first in importance is, 'Listen, Israel: The Lord your God is one; so love the Lord God with all your passion and prayer and intelligence and energy.' And here is the second: 'Love others as well as you love yourself.' There is no other commandment that ranks with these." (Mark 12:29–31 MSG)

When we do the first commandment, the second commandment gets easier. What are specific ways you can practice loving the Lord God with all your passion, purpose, intelligence, and energy?

Do we really care for others the way God wants us to show love and have that same measurement of loving acts toward ourselves? Evaluate.

Do you love yourself well? Look past that quote in the Bible verse to the final sentence. There is no other commandment that is as important as these two commands. How many times have we placed something in higher priority than loving God, loving others, and loving self?

Keep in mind that love is more than an emotion; it's a series of actions.

One way others know we love them is when we are consistent in our care for them. With that same principle, what needs to change for you to be consistent in your care for self?

But Jesus often withdrew to the wilderness for prayer. (Luke 5:16)

Sometimes when we take a timeout from helping others to take care of ourselves, we feel guilty. In this passage, it says Jesus often withdrew. And he was JESUS! If he took time to withdraw and rest, how much more do we, as mere humans, need that too?

Notice the word *often*. It wasn't a one-time thing. Who did he withdraw from?

Jesus went to the wilderness. Why do you think he chose that place for his self-care?

What did Jesus do during his timeout? He prayed. How will prayer help you make the most of your withdrawal from others? Prayer is the ultimate spirit-care.

Dear friend, I hope all is well with you and that you are as healthy in body as you are strong in spirit. (3 John 1:2)

This note was written from the apostle John to Gaius. What did John hope for Gaius?

Imagine God writing to you, "I hope all is well with you." What does "all is well" look like in your life?

Or maybe you're more likely to say, "All is *not* well with me." Self-care helps you address that.

Notice the importance of self-care from this passage. How can it help you be healthy in body and strong in spirit?

Jesus replied, "'You must love the LORD your God with all your heart, all your soul, and all your mind.' This is the first and greatest commandment."
(Matthew 22:37–38)

Let's offer God our best self, our whole self. This means we have to take *care* of self.

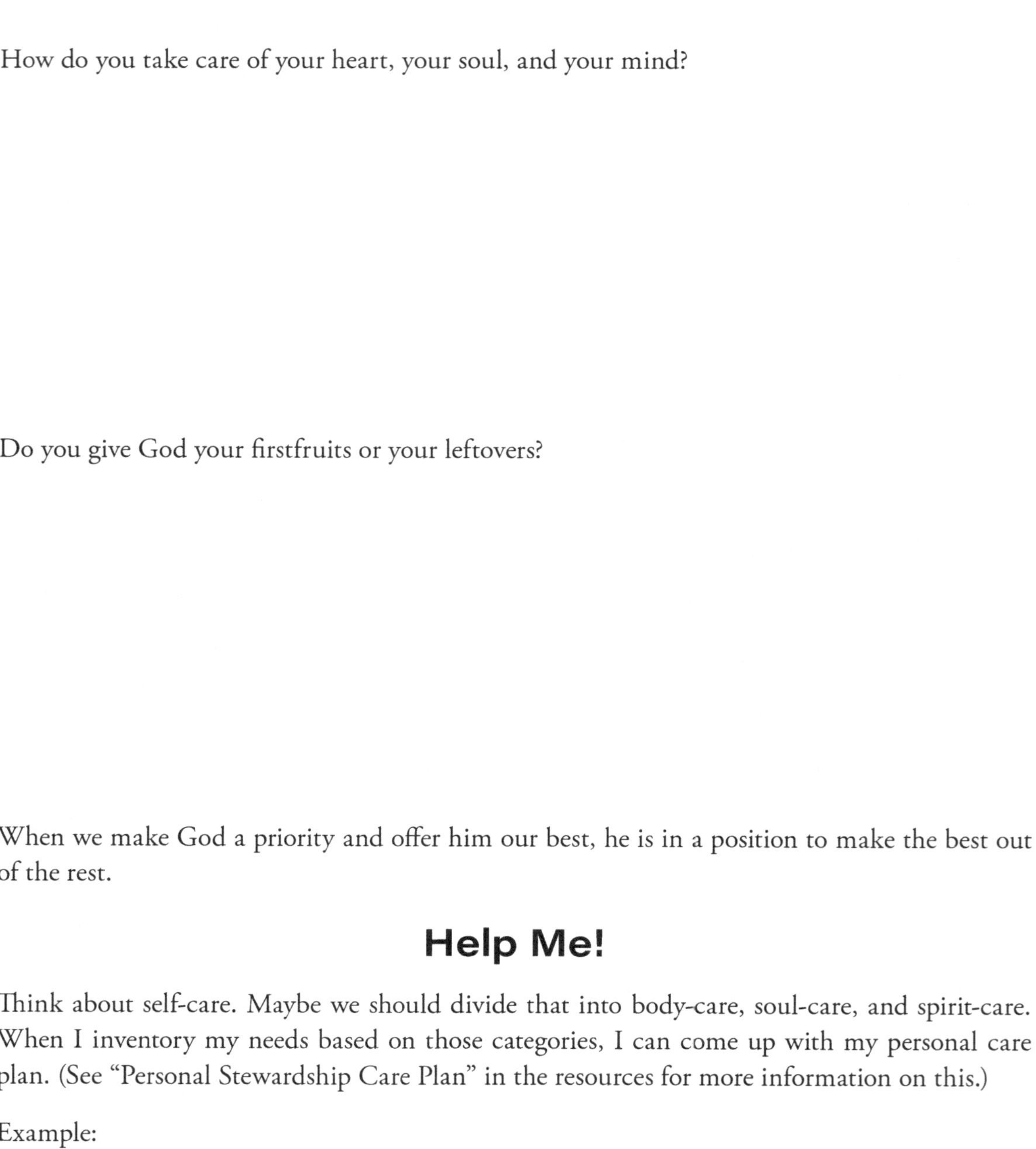

How do you take care of your heart, your soul, and your mind?

Do you give God your firstfruits or your leftovers?

When we make God a priority and offer him our best, he is in a position to make the best out of the rest.

Help Me!

Think about self-care. Maybe we should divide that into body-care, soul-care, and spirit-care. When I inventory my needs based on those categories, I can come up with my personal care plan. (See "Personal Stewardship Care Plan" in the resources for more information on this.)

Example:

Body-care

- Get a pedicure to take care of excessive callous build-up. Enjoy the relaxing experience as well as the joy of having polished toenails.

- Take a nap in the middle of the day. Yes, you're allowed!
- Take an exercise class designed for your level of fitness.

Soul-care

- Write in your journal to process whatever is weighing you down.
- Inventory reasons to celebrate. (Sometimes we focus so much on the negative, we forget that positive things are happening all the time.)
- Spend time in a creative outlet, using a gift, talent, or hobby you sometimes neglect.
- Watch a movie with a friend (in person or via a watch party).

Spirit-care

- Devote uninterrupted time to have a conversation with God that involves more than a list of wishes.
- Make a date with yourself and your Bible to study God's character.
- Watch worship music that has a lyric video with it. Focus on the words.

I have a friend who regularly reminds me to advocate for my needs. She encourages me to speak up when others don't notice something that seems obvious. We can't assume others see our needs. If it's good to be brave and represent something that is weighing heavy on us, isn't it just as important to be that same advocate for self *with* self? We must give ourselves permission to slow down and do maintenance before we have a breakdown.

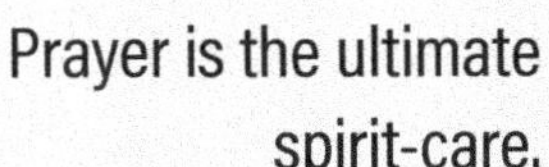

This isn't just about physical caretaking and pampering. It's what goes deeper—to the soul level.

John Wesley was known to ask, "How is it with your soul?" Many of us resonate with an old hymn called "It Is Well with My Soul." Why does this song minister to us? It delivers a sense of calm and peace. Sometimes we need to be reminded that it *can* be well with our souls.

"Soul care begins with this one premise: I must create space for my soul to thrive."[3] This concept really speaks to me! In fact, I'm writing this on a sticky note right now. (See section on "Margin" to address this further.)

As we've discussed in other sections, one way to look at making total wellbeing a priority is to see it as personal stewardship. Use the resources God has given you to make sure you're taking care of the temple and your inner being—body, soul, and spirit.

Ask yourself: How does God want me to take care of myself right now?

Homework

1. Get out your calendar app and schedule self-care for body, soul, and spirit.
2. Cancel one repeating obligation on your schedule that no longer fits with your purpose and passion. You need to make space for personal care.
3. Read "Self-Care / Soul Care" in the resource section.
4. What struggles have you had this week? List them and brainstorm ways to prevent or overcome them moving forward.

Health Check

Body: What is my plan to listen to what my body needs this week so I don't neglect it?

Soul: How will I add grace space for my soul this week?

Spirit: What is one example from this past week when my heart was overwhelmed and I remembered to run to God first?

What does "all is well" look like in your life?

Hurrahs and Happy Dances

List your victories from the week and celebrate them. Share them with one of your cheerleaders. Note any aha! moments from this week.

Hope Quest

Father, I'm starting to get it. You want me to take care of myself so that I am around to take care of others. Help me make time for it and not feel guilty advocating for my needs.

EQUIPPED FOR WELLBEING

Just as we have needs built inside each of us, God supplies us with the provision for those needs. He has solutions for our challenges. Often, we endure a struggle God never meant for us to allow in our lives. Other times, we tough it out on our own rather than relying on God for a way to escape it or to bear it.

We all struggle differently, but we all have struggles. As I've coached others, I see how common it is to allow trials and circumstances to derail wellbeing intentions. Just as I want to equip them with tools to be successful, I know God, our ultimate life coach, equips us with what we need to live as he intended.

How can we overcome so many different struggles? Does God expect us to? In this chapter, we will look at how God equips us for wellbeing.

Heartstrings

I like homes that have built-ins. Bungalows have these wonderful built-in bookcases and china cabinets. Prairie School style homes often have butler pantries. Mid-century modern features a bar area perfect for a beverage center. No matter the architectural style, built-ins are created for both function and beauty.

We are like those homes. God builds inside of us all we need to function and to be beautiful. He equips us with what we need for wellbeing. What is our part in accessing those built-ins?

This year more than ever, I'm looking for something to change, and I need God's direction. With so much outside of my control, it's nice to find a few ways I can make a difference, starting inside myself. I want to utilize God's built-ins for function and for beauty.

God builds inside of us all we need to function and to be beautiful.

God is impressing on me to focus on personal stewardship through seeking wellbeing. Don't get me wrong. I'm not saying if I do my part that God is going to heal the things outside of my control. He does heal, but he often uses us broken. Regardless, he desires that I take care of the only body, soul, and spirit I get on this earth.

It's reassuring to know we can have abundant life—an existence even better than we can possibly dream up. God designed our lives to be enjoyed. It must break his heart when we allow so much stress to overwhelm our days. What does abundant mean? I like the sound of this: *to the full, till it overflows* (John 10:10 AMPC). Yes! I want *that* kind of life.

Heavenly Insights

By his divine power, God has given us everything we need for living a godly life. We have received all of this by coming to know him, the one who called us to himself by means of his marvelous glory and excellence. (2 Peter 1:3)

We may feel inadequate, unworthy, or unprepared, but God will never abandon us where he leads us. His presence will be with us, and his power will equip us. This includes our focus on wellbeing.

Part of godly living is choosing a life of wellbeing in body, soul, and spirit.

God (with his divine power, which is superior to our insufficient human power) has given us everything we need for wellbeing.

What is your favorite phrase in this passage?

> *All Scripture is inspired by God and is useful to teach us what is true and to make us realize what is wrong in our lives. It corrects us when we are wrong and teaches us to do what is right. God uses it to prepare and equip his people to do every good work.* (2 Timothy 3:16–17)

Look up this passage in the Amplified Bible. Write it out here.

What is the Bible designed to do in our lives?

What is the result of God using Scripture in our lives?

How is pursuing wellbeing of body, soul, and spirit "good work"?

What do you feel is missing for you to be able to succeed at wellbeing?

According to this passage, is it really missing? (Either the missing element is *not* needed for wellbeing and is merely an excuse, or it *is* needed, and we have access to that kind of help from God.)

> *Now may the God of peace—who brought up from the dead our Lord Jesus, the great Shepherd of the sheep, and ratified an eternal covenant with his blood—may he equip you with all you need for doing his will. May he produce in you, through the power of Jesus Christ, every good thing that is pleasing to him. All glory to him forever and ever! Amen.* (Hebrews 13:20–21)

Read this passage in the ESV and the AMPC for added meaning.

What stands out to you from this passage, using the various versions to see the nuances of wording, that might propel your success with wellbeing?

How does a motive of pleasing God help you pursue wellbeing?

What wellbeing motives do you have that are not in alignment with his will?

Ears that hear and eyes that see—we get our basic equipment from GOD*!*
(Proverbs 20:12 MSG)

What do hearing and seeing have to do with how God equips us?

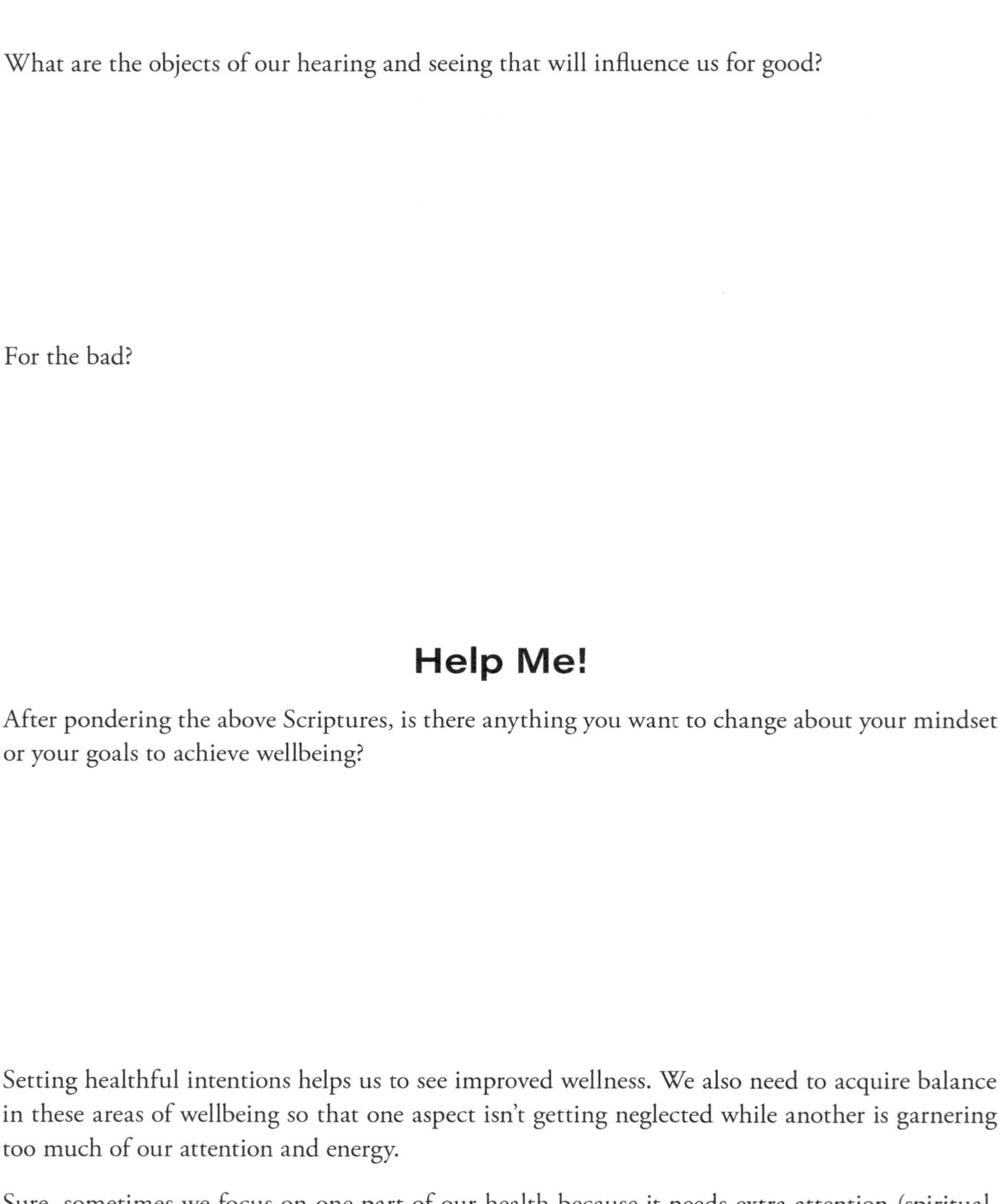

What are the objects of our hearing and seeing that will influence us for good?

For the bad?

Help Me!

After pondering the above Scriptures, is there anything you want to change about your mindset or your goals to achieve wellbeing?

Setting healthful intentions helps us to see improved wellness. We also need to acquire balance in these areas of wellbeing so that one aspect isn't getting neglected while another is garnering too much of our attention and energy.

Sure, sometimes we focus on one part of our health because it needs extra attention (spiritual, physical, mental, social, emotional). But we have to be mindful not to let that high priority cause us to overlook what the rest of our being needs for wellness. While a good steward takes care of her resources, she is not empowered for optimal results if she fixates on one aspect and abuses or neglects other responsibilities.

Every chapter in the homework section, I encourage you to identify the struggles you have had that week. The practice is to list the struggles and then brainstorm ways to prevent or overcome them moving forward. This is a great way to learn to manage your issues.

If you are having a hard time thinking of ways to do this, take it a step further. Imagine you're talking to a friend who has those problems, and you have the answers. What advice would we give them? This approach moves past self-pity and gets to the viewpoint of resolution. It's too easy to allow a victim mentality to sneak in when we can't get victory over a circumstance. Yet we know from this chapter's Bible study that God equips us with everything we need to have wellbeing. So, what is the missing element in the equation? Do you ever find your mind or heart saying, "Kathy, you don't understand. My case is different. I'm just a victim of my circumstances."

What can you think or do differently to find your way out of that mindset?

Or maybe you don't have a victim mentality, but you are dealing with other struggles. Are these situations outside your control or within your control to change?

I'm reevaluating where I'm at in my pursuit of wellbeing, and I'm sharing these questions with you in case you're ready to revamp your plan along with me.

Questions I'm asking:

- What does optimal physical health look like for me, even if God doesn't heal my "chronics"?

- What are "sure things" to help with physical health that are non-negotiables toward physical wellbeing?

- What have been my excuses for not taking care of these things?

- What are some other ideas that might help with progress?

- What will help me have the "want to"? How can I find joy or satisfaction in it?

- What can I reduce timewise in my schedule to give me more white space and energy to focus on wellbeing?

- What can I do to jumpstart my new dedication?

- What worked before that I can implement again? Why did I stop it? What can I do to make sure I keep with it this time?

- What worked before that I can't do now? What can I substitute for it?

- What are my challenges to success?

- What would make me feel my best?

- What can I research if I'm not sure?

Questions to ask nightly:

- How did today's choices affect my spiritual wellbeing?
- How did today's choices affect my emotional/mental wellbeing?
- How did today's choices affect my physical wellbeing?
- Did I honor and glorify God with my choices?
- Is there something I want to do better next time?
- What did I learn from today that will help me moving forward?
- How can I apply grace to my soul right now so I have sweet surrender and sleep?

Homework

1. Spend some time answering and journaling the questions in the Help Me! section.
2. Create a card or computer screen/phone sticky that asks the nightly questions above. Or use the wellbeing planner that goes with this book. Review them each night before bedtime.
3. What struggles have you had this week? List them and brainstorm ways to prevent or overcome them moving forward.

Health Check

Body: If God equips me with everything I need for life, what help is he making available for me to take care of my physical health?

Soul: As I do an inner-being inventory of God's built-in tools, what resources will help with my will? (Will: a strong determination to do something or not do something.) What does it take to utilize these resources?

Spirit: What will I do this week to grow closer to God and help me have abundant life?

We can have abundant life—an existence even better than we can possibly dream up.

Hurrahs and Happy Dances

List your victories from the week and celebrate them. Share them with one of your cheerleaders. Note any aha! moments from this week.

Hope Quest

Father, Son, and Holy Spirit, I thank you for equipping me with everything I need. Father, you know my needs before I even tell them to you. Jesus, thank you for paying the price on the cross so that I can come to the throne of grace with boldness in prayer. Holy Spirit, give me discernment for the changes I need to make this week.

THOSE DREADED PLATEAUS

This progress, performance, perfection, productivity gal despises plateaus! (How's that for alliteration?) What does it mean to hit a plateau? A plateau is merely a state of little or no change following a period of activity or progress. We are programmed to expect progress in exchange for productivity, and when that doesn't happen, it feels like failure.

Tracy Winkler said, "Plateaus are the places where your initial zeal is drying up and your vision for the finish line is fading."[4]

Sometimes plateaus are warning signs that if something doesn't change, a person will become complacent or even stagnant. They aren't toxic but lead to choices that can create toxic situations if we allow them. So, let's use plateaus as red flags warning us to give attention and take action to prevent neglect.

Since we are all about body, soul, and spirit, let's discuss the plateaus we all experience from time to time in each of those categories.

Heartstrings

Plateaus remind me there is more outside of my control than within it. I can be making all the right choices for my physical goals with diet, exercise, rest, and more. I see good outcomes for a while. It feels good. The results seem like a reward for being intentional with good priorities and discipline. Then it happens. No more measurable outcomes to give me positive reinforcement. Following the same program but not seeing the same results.

We bemoan the misery of hitting a plateau, but there are times that a plateau is a good thing.

I wrote this in my manuscript for a future book about waiting:

> The wait is not a delay, it's an on-purpose plateau to let what *used to be* catch up with what's *going to be* in the future. It's just like losing weight. If we don't allow for the plateaus when we diet, our skin won't shrink up as well, and we walk around like Shar Pei puppies. We don't want saggy baggy skin, and we don't want saggy baggy lives, either. A life on hold isn't a life delayed. It's just not time yet.

When I was a young adult, my spiritual leaders taught me that if there was ever a time I had felt closer to God than currently, it meant I was now backslidden. They gave no allowance for a plateau. They discussed the hot, cold, or lukewarm status found in Revelation, and two of those were sinful. As I ponder that teaching, I see that their belief bases our position in Christ on how we *feel* rather than on his love and the price he paid to redeem us.

Plateaus are a stage of life, just as much as growth stages. Even though it seems as if nothing is happening during a plateau, there are things going on under the surface. Some for the good, some not so good. Just as cells regenerate or die, our inner being is renewing or declining. Is there a third option? I'm not sure. But I know God uses the wait as much as he uses the go and the grow.

Heavenly Insights

The Bible talks about milk and meat to nourish the believer and facilitate growth. Both are important at the right time. When a believer who is ready to advance to meat doesn't dig in to grow, they experience a plateau. Growth happens during a theological term called sanctification. It is a cooperative effort between the Lord at work through the Spirit and our response to his work by being diligent in exercising growth of spirit and soul. It takes spiritual meat and daily determination to practice what we learn and not just store it up as knowledge.

But I have this against you, that you have abandoned the love you had at first.
(Revelation 2:4 ESV)

In this warning to the Ephesus church, John mentions that they have lost their first love. This love happened when they first fell in love with Jesus and when they put their love of Jesus first in their lives.

The ESV uses the word *abandoned*, as if the status of not being as close to God is caused by a choice to leave the relationship. Other versions use the word *lost,* as if maybe it wasn't intentional but neglected and overlooked. These are probably two causes to the same condition.

What can you do to make sure you do not experience this sort of spiritual plateau?

A life on hold isn't a life delayed. It's just not time yet.

You have been believers so long now that you ought to be teaching others. Instead, you need someone to teach you again the basic things about God's word. You are like babies who need milk and cannot eat solid food. (Hebrews 5:12)

This sounds a lot like a parent scolding an errant child, doesn't it? It isn't a comfortable thought. But let's stay uncomfortable for just a moment longer and ask ourselves, "Where am I in my spiritual growth process?"

The ideal goal is to always be learning through mentors and, at the same time, always have someone we mentor.

> *But I press on to possess that perfection for which Christ Jesus first possessed me. No, dear brothers and sisters, I have not achieved it, but I focus on this one thing: Forgetting the past and looking forward to what lies ahead, I press on to reach the end of the race and receive the heavenly prize for which God, through Christ Jesus, is calling us.* (Philippians 3:12–14)

This description from Paul reveals what to do during a plateau, or sometimes, even to prevent one.

What do you need to forget about your past when it comes to wellbeing of body, soul, and spirit?

Where do you need to fix your focus as you press on toward the goal?

> *Brothers and sisters, we urge you to warn those who are lazy. Encourage those who are timid. Take tender care of those who are weak. Be patient with everyone.* (1 Thessalonians 5:14)

Sometimes plateaus happen because we get idle with our priorities (or, I should say, *lack* of healthful priorities).

We need to do all the action steps found in this passage with ourselves (not just with others). This becomes a form of self-care and soul-care. Practice self-talk that warns against laziness. Give yourself encouragement, tender loving care, and patience.

Help Me!

When we hit a plateau, wellbeing coaches tell us to be patient and stay consistent. But if it continues for more than six weeks, they recommend we change up our program. It's hard to know when to stay consistent with the same program and when it's time to change it up! That goes for any form of wellbeing, not just physical.

> *"Keep on asking, and you will receive what you ask for. Keep on seeking, and you will find. Keep on knocking, and the door will be opened to you. For everyone who asks, receives. Everyone who seeks, finds. And to everyone who knocks, the door will be opened."* (Matthew 7:7–8)

- Plateaus give us the choice to keep on or to give up and quit.
- What will you keep on doing? Asking. Seeking. Knocking.
- What will you get in return? Eventually—results!

How do you break through a spiritual plateau?

- First, make sure you anchor your thoughts on Christ's love and the price he paid to redeem us, rather than your feelings about your spiritual maturity. A plateau doesn't cause you to lose being a child of God.
- Make spiritual growth a priority. What helps you grow?

- What rejuvenates your faith when it has become stale?

- Try reading a new devotional, and journal your thoughts through it.
- Select a book of the Bible to read through. Write your insights. Add to your growth by reading a Bible commentary or other version/paraphrase of the passage.
- Use different colors of pens/pencils. Mark your Bible to coordinate with different themes.

How do you break through a soul plateau?

- Your inner being needs special attention too. If there were a soul spa, what would refresh you?

- Self-talk needs to be renovated.
- Evaluate if any seed of bitterness, jealousy, judgmentalism, or pride has entered in.

How do you break through a physical plateau?

- Look over your program and see if you've let up in any area. Maybe your serving sizes have grown slightly larger. Or your macros (fats, carbs, proteins) are out of balance for how your body best functions. Or maybe you're still exercising but not really breaking a sweat. Sometimes we say we are still on program when really, we've let something slip.
- Decide if it's best to stick with your current program or time to change up the program with something new. Often, we just need consistency and patience in what we are doing. Other times, we need to make changes. Just like how our muscles can grow accustomed to a workout program and require new exercises to be challenged, our physical wellbeing program periodically needs to be updated.

In order to address a plateau of any kind, change something that has become stale. It's like driving a different route to work—you get a different viewpoint. (Read "The Problem with Plateaus Is . . ." in the resource section.)

Homework

Whether it's preventive maintenance or corrective attention, let's apply the principles discussed in the above section.

1. What one step will you take to prevent/address a spiritual plateau?

2. What one step will you take to prevent/address a soul plateau?

3. What one step will you take to prevent/address a physical plateau?

4. What struggles have you had this week? List them and brainstorm ways to prevent or overcome them moving forward.

Health Check

Body: Where have I slipped in my physical wellbeing program?

Soul: Who is my mentor? Who am I mentoring? Is it time to make contact again?

Spirit: What is my next step to make sure my spiritual growth doesn't stagnate?

God uses the wait as much as he uses the go and the grow.

Hurrahs and Happy Dances

List your victories from the week and celebrate them. Share them with one of your cheerleaders. Note any aha! moments from this week.

Hope Quest

O Father! When I first came to faith in you because of Jesus, I had so much zeal. There was a spiritual growth spurt. But as life happens, I sometimes plateau. Help me know what to do in that pause—to either rest and refresh in you or to revive in my attitudes and actions. I don't want to stall out or stagnate. Help me finish strong.

BUSY SYNDROME

One of the biggest first world problems we deal with today is fighting the *busy syndrome*. We almost see it as a status symbol. When people ask us how we're doing, we answer with, "Oh, I'm staying busy!" Perhaps we need to quit asking about the doing part and ask how they are being. We are human *beings* after all!

It reminds me of a quote from Corrie ten Boom. "If the devil cannot make us bad, he will make us busy."[5]

How will we truly rest in the Lord if we don't slow down enough to focus on him? It's like whirling on a merry-go-round and trying to have a conversation with someone who is standing on the ground next to the ride.

Heartstrings

When I fidgeted as a child, I didn't like how Mom told me to be still, and I still don't like having to slow down. But I understand why our heavenly Father chooses to nurture us during those times we willingly rest. God isn't scolding us when he says, "Be still." He wants to refresh us!

I created an allegory from Mark 4:35–41:

> I was tired from doing much to serve alongside Jesus, so he encouraged me to take a boat trip with him. Others came for the ride. To be honest, I was tired of the crowds and wished it were just Jesus and me.
>
> I enjoy a good boat outing . . . until bad weather comes. Add in wind, rain, and choppy water. That isn't my idea of taking a break. My heart fluttered—but Jesus slept. *He slept!* Didn't he comprehend the danger we were in?
>
> I cried out to him, and he instantly quieted the wind and told the sea, "Peace! Be still!" All at once, a great calm surrounded me externally, but even better, it infused me internally. I realized then that it's silly to fear the very things God created (like raging storms). He had control over creation at the beginning and is still in charge today. That's when it hit me. I have a choice. Do I tremble in fear because of his power, or do I join the winds and the rain and decide to be still and accept his peace?

Heavenly Insights

Be still in the presence of the Lord, and wait patiently for him to act. Don't worry about evil people who prosper or fret about their wicked schemes. (Psalm 37:7)

It sounds relaxing to be still in a spa setting or as a couch potato (and those are fine), but God has something else in mind. How do you go about being still in his presence?

How can you be still with your body, soul, and spirit?

It's hard to be busy and be still at the same time. Maybe that's why the next part of the verse says to "wait patiently for him to act." Does something in your life need a little less *busy* and a lot more *be still*?

"Don't worry" in the above verse gives good advice on how to be still in soul and spirit. When you trust God by waiting, you gain peace and lose fear. Psalm 37 mentions a specific worry about those who are evil, but we can expand that to any worry. What is worrying you right now?

It is useless for you to work so hard from early morning until late at night, anxiously working for food to eat; for God gives rest to his loved ones. (Psalm 127:2)

When you need rest, how productive is your work?

God isn't scolding us when he says, "Be still." He wants to refresh us!

You can't rest when you are anxious or worried about provisions. Ask me how I know. No really. Ask me. It's because the Bible say so!

It helps to know God gives rest to those he loves. Does God love you? Of course, he does. Rest in that!

Then Jesus said, "Come to me, all of you who are weary and carry heavy burdens, and I will give you rest. Take my yoke upon you. Let me teach you, because I am humble and gentle at heart, and you will find rest for your souls. For my yoke is easy to bear, and the burden I give you is light." (Matthew 11:28–30)

One thing about Jesus coming to earth as a human—he understands our struggles. Here he mentions those of us who are weary and burdened down. He knows just what we need. He offers to give us rest.

What does it take to enter into his rest?

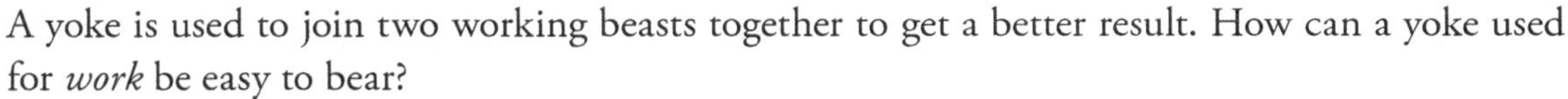

A yoke is used to join two working beasts together to get a better result. How can a yoke used for *work* be easy to bear?

Don't worry if you don't know how to yoke up with the Savior—he says he will teach you. What kind of teacher is he?

Help Me!

Are we too busy to slow down? Often, we say, "When [thus-and-so] happens, then I will catch up on my rest." For you, that might be one of these:

- When I finish that project.
- When I get that promotion/raise.
- When I find a different job.
- When I have enough money to hire help.
- When my kids leave home.
- When my finances improve.
- When I get in better health/shape.
- When I retire.

Unfortunately, the less margin we have in our schedule, the more mistakes we make. We can't rest, so our minds take twice as long to do the work. I'm reminded of the anonymous quote, "The hurrier I go, the behinder I get." The opposite of the quote is true too. If I am rested and take an optimal pace with my work, it seems as if I can get more done in less amount of time.

A story is told of two woodchoppers who challenged each other to split wood for eight hours, and at the end of the time, see who had the largest woodpile. Every hour, one chopper took a break. The other went nonstop, thinking the extra time would amount to a larger woodpile. To him, it meant easy victory.

At eight hours, there was only one obvious winner. The one who took breaks had a much larger woodpile. The losing contestant asked, "How can this be? I worked the entire time, while you took a break every hour."

The winner responded, "I used that time to sharpen the ax!"

The problem with staying too busy is we strive for extra pay, praise, performance, power, or perfection. We will never rest if we chase these self-focused goals. Let's lay down those pursuits and chase after just one thing. More of Jesus. Then our hearts can find rest.

Consider how Pastor J.D. Greear puts it.

> Let's face it: sometimes going "all the way" with Jesus is a challenge, and we find ourselves lagging behind where we feel like we should be. In times like these, it might make sense to tell ourselves to work a little harder, to devote ourselves more fully to God. But the gospel diagnoses things differently. Ironically, the gospel tells us that when following Jesus gets difficult, the answer is not to "work harder" but to "rest better." Only by learning to rest in Jesus will we have the strength we need to thrive.[6]

Do you tend to busy yourself so your mind is distracted from worry? What will it take for you to be still in God's presence and wait for him to act?

1. I will set aside ______________ to focus more on God.
2. I will deny my tendency to stress so I can fully rest.
3. I will focus my thoughts on God—not on the problems. I will trust his process. *You will keep in perfect peace, all who trust in you, all whose thoughts are fixed on you!* (Isaiah 26:3).
4. I will find a relaxing atmosphere away from the clutter of life to rest. *Rest in the shade of this tree while water is brought to wash your feet.* (Genesis 18:4).

Homework

1. Read "Balancing Priorities" and "Margin" in the resource section.
2. Listen to a song that sings about *peace.* Focus on the lyrics. What song did you select?
3. Before you write your to-do list, take time with the Lord.
4. Ask the Lord to order your steps so that you aren't spinning your wheels.
5. What struggles have you had this week? List them and brainstorm ways to prevent or overcome them moving forward.

Health Check

Body: What do I catch myself mindlessly doing instead of placing my entire body in a posture of stillness?

Soul: What is interfering with my ability to have calmness in mind and heart?

Spirit: How is my busyness harming my intimacy with God?

Want rest? Lay down other pursuits and chase after just one thing. More of Jesus.

Hurrahs and Happy Dances

List your victories from the week and celebrate them. Share them with one of your cheerleaders. Note any aha! moments from this week.

Hope Quest

Father, reveal to me the needless busyness in my life. Help me sort it out so I can be still in your presence. Show me the worries I need to hand over to you. I catch myself striving instead of having a restful peace of mind. I receive your refreshing—enough to hold me through the day.

THE HEART OF THE MATTER

In this chapter, we continue to explore how to find wellbeing where it counts forever—that invisible part of us that goes to heaven when we die. Wellbeing happens when we put God first. Struggles flare up when we get that priority out of order, and they also happen when we focus more on performance than on relationship. Our hearts are designed to love and be loved.

It's a deep concept to investigate wholeness of heart and soul, but that doesn't give us permission to not think about it. Let's dig in and see what the Bible says and how it applies to living a life of wellbeing. But first, a story.

Heartstrings

When I see the words *heart and soul,* I think of the old jazz tune by the same name. I remember someone teaching me how to play the easy part of the duet. After I proved I had it down and could play it on my own, she sat down by me and played the complicated notes and rhythms. Considering at that point in life, I'd never had a piano lesson, I was thrilled to make music. All it took was having a more experienced player duet with me.

Isn't that the same with the heart and soul of our inner beings? Father God gives us music. With it, we can manage to play a simple tune in life. It might sound a bit rudimentary. But then along comes Jesus the Maestro and makes all the difference in our lives. Then the Holy Spirit fills us while filling the music with intricate melodies and rhythms that turns an elementary tune into a classical performance.

How does God make a difference to the wellbeing of my heart and soul? Am I willing to play my simple tune and leave the complicated details to him? Do I mess up my part by trying to do his part? Do I relish the experience of playing together as much as the goal of completing the song?

As we examine the Bible verses addressing the heart of the matter, let's keep one thing in focus—God is the one at work in us and through us. We're not alone on the piano bench of life.

Heavenly Insights

Guard your heart above all else, for it determines the course of your life.
(Proverbs 4:23)

What does it mean to guard your heart?

How do you keep vigilant watch over it?

How does the heart determine the course of your life?

Trust in the LORD with all your heart; do not depend on your own understanding. Seek his will in all you do, and he will show you which path to take. (Proverbs 3:5–6)

The word *trust* means to rely confidently on. Lean on. How do you trust in the Lord?

What are some examples of thoughts and actions that displayed this trust?

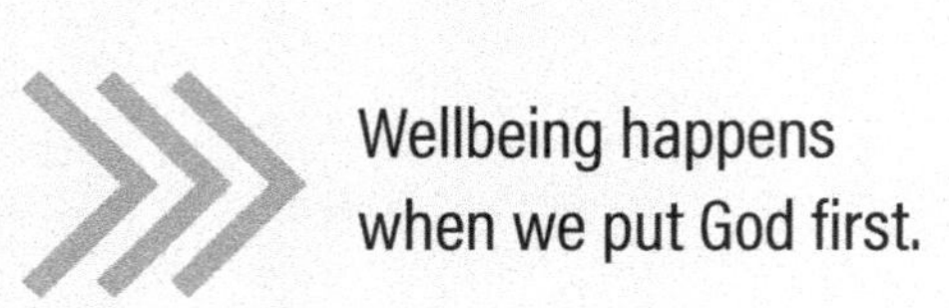

How do you trust in the Lord *with all your heart?* Hold nothing back!

When we don't depend on our own understanding, we're in a good position to trust God. It's when we try to do life on our own ("I do it myself") that we get into trouble. Some of us tend to do what we can on our own first and not bother God with it—saving our access to him for the big things in our lives. But everything in our lives is small stuff to God! (He recognizes it is significant to us, so it matters to him. Yet, it's simple for him to manage for us because he's a big God.)

What happens when you set aside your self-reliance and depend on God to direct your steps?

How can you recognize God's voice and sense his direction and purpose for your life? How do you differentiate his voice from your own thoughts?

Heart/soul/mind trilogy

Read Matthew 22:37 and Mark 12:30. These passages in the New Testament are taken from the principle Moses taught in Deuteronomy 6:5.

> *The man answered, "You must love the LORD your God with all your heart, all your soul, all your strength, and all your mind."* (Luke 10:27)

This passage is mentioned in three of the four gospels. It is missing in the gospel of John. I find that interesting, considering John probably had the deepest connection with Jesus and was keenly aware of the importance of this heart/soul/mind/strength focus as a healthful priority.

Matthew only mentions heart, soul, and mind. Mark and Luke add in the word *strength*. This kind of strength is also interpreted *power*, *might*, and *ability*.[7] Strength adds the physical component (body) to heart, soul, and mind, which reflect the inner being. When I consider that Luke was a physician, it makes sense that he references the body.

The primary command is to love the Lord with our complete being. True love encompasses an *all-in* mentality. Is there anything regarding your heart, soul, strength, or mind that isn't fully loving God?

Why are you holding it back?

What will happen to your relationship with the Lord as you relinquish control?

Extra reading:

- Deuteronomy 4:29
- Joshua 22:5

Help Me!

How can we take steps toward having an all-in mentality with our hearts and souls?

Is it God's voice?

- In the last section, I challenged you to determine if the thoughts in your mind and heart are coming from God, Satan, or yourself. How do you do that?

- God's voice doesn't shame or scold us.
- God's voice aligns with his character and his Word (the Bible).

- When I position myself as a sheep and God as my Shepherd, I will recognize his voice.
- The main thing is, am I really listening for it?

Steps to heart-and-soul peace

Live life in Christ Jesus and let go of what holds you back. God will grant peace, and that peace is what is available to guard your heart and mind. *Don't worry about anything; instead, pray about everything. Tell God what you need and thank him for all he has done. Then you will experience God's peace, which exceeds anything we can understand. His peace will guard your hearts and minds as you live in Christ Jesus* (Philippians 4:6–7).

1. **Go on a worry fast.** Each time a worry surfaces in your mind, learn how to replace it with prayer and biblical self-talk.
2. **Pray with petitions and praises.** Petitions are those specific requests we confide to God. (I tell my friends I pray with TMI, but God doesn't see it that way. He loves to hear from me—too much information and all!) Let God know your concerns but also focus on praising him. Worship displaces worry.
3. **Focus on God's attributes.** When you read Scripture, search for a virtue or role of God—a characteristic trait. Hint: usually, this is something I value about God that I can't attain 100 percent in my humanness. Choose one attribute to focus on as you praise him during your personal worship time.

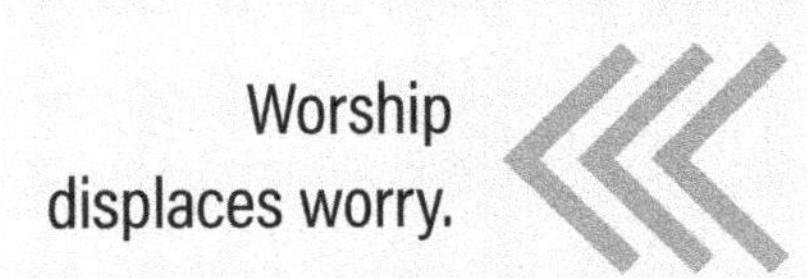

4. **Sense God's wholeness as you absorb his peace.** This peace is different than manmade peace. It contributes to heart-and-soul wellbeing. It quiets the upset and delivers rest, sort of like an antacid calms heartburn.

Search God with all your heart

> *For I know the thoughts that I think toward you, says the Lord, thoughts of peace and not of evil, to give you a future and a hope. Then you will call upon Me and go and pray to Me, and I will listen to you. And you will seek Me and find Me, when you search for Me with all your heart.* (Jeremiah 29:11–13 NKJV)

The above passage was a conversation between God and Jeremiah. While it isn't a promise for today, we can extrapolate from this passage the heart God has for his children. With that in mind, let's focus on steps we can take to make God number one.

1. **Call on God.** When you pray, God listens. To personalize it, pause long enough to see if God has anything to add to the prayer conversation.
2. **Seek God.** When you seek God with all your heart, you will assuredly find him. Not simply in a generic way, but in a personal, life-changing way.
3. **Make this search a priority.** *The Message* in verse 13 says: *Yes, when you get serious about finding me and want it more than anything else, I'll make sure you won't be disappointed.*

A worry fast

Let's ponder the idea of fasting from worry. Just as some use a food fast to detox the body and bring spiritual and physical health, a worry fast can create a healthier environment for our hearts and minds. What intake contributes to your mental diet? What are the ingredients that contribute to your worries?

Get to the root cause of them, not simply the surface concerns. Keep in mind the perceived worry is often not the real problem, so be willing to go deep with this. Once you've addressed them, let them go so you can have a worry-free time for your fast.

A worry date

A counselor advised a friend of mine to limit her time worrying. She had an appointment with her worries at a certain time each day and was restricted to that time slot. Just fifteen minutes. Any other time of day, she mentally told herself, "It isn't time to think about that right now. At 6:00 p.m. you can focus on those thoughts." She found that when her date with worry came, she didn't have as many fearful or negative thoughts hitting her right then, and she could move on without those burdens bogging down her emotions.

Homework

1. Figure out a journaling method that works for you. In this journal, chronicle your talks with God. Note your lightbulb moments—the insights God gives you.
2. Consider going on a worry fast or implementing a worry date. How long will it last? How will you put your worries in check when they surface?
3. What struggles have you had this week? List them and brainstorm ways to prevent or overcome them moving forward.

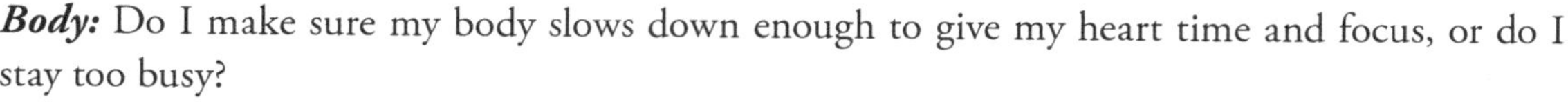

Health Check

Body: Do I make sure my body slows down enough to give my heart time and focus, or do I stay too busy?

Soul: Is there something on my heart right now that is keeping me from being able to say, "It is well with my soul"?

Spirit: When was the last time I searched God with all my heart? What am I holding back?

Hurrahs and Happy Dances

List your victories from the week and celebrate them. Share them with one of your cheerleaders. Note any aha! moments from this week.

Hope Quest

Father, with my whole heart I come to you. My soul longs for your presence. I yield my mind and strength to your use. Meet me where I am, but don't leave me where you find me. Make yourself at home in my heart.

CURB YOUR ATTITUDES AND ACTIONS

Rather than learning to curb our *appetites*, what would happen if we learned to curb our *attitudes* and *actions*? Curb as a verb means: control, limit, restrict, restrain, reduce, hold back, rein in, and cut back.[8]

My wellbeing choices are affected by how I'm feeling. When I'm weary, it's especially hard to curb my attitudes and actions.

One of my biggest struggles is when I'm exhausted. I push myself too hard while working toward achieving life goals and serving others. I don't rest enough. There isn't enough relaxation time to unwind. I carry burdens for others so long that they seem like my own. I'm exhausted. Oh, wait, I already said that. See? I'm a hot mess!

Let's not sleepwalk through life on autopilot because we're in the fog of fatigue and frustrations. I want to curb my attitudes and actions. I bet you do too. Join me in doing this together.

Heartstrings

I get disappointed in myself when I don't have the dedication and discipline needed to choose the best wellbeing options for personal stewardship. Making healthy choices feels like work—and when I'm too drained, I don't want to add one more thing on my to-do list.

One struggle is the difference between law/legalism versus grace/freedom. I don't want to be down on myself when I fail to live up to my personal stewardship intentions. But I don't want to be so loosey-goosey that I slip back into pre-wellbeing days.

Personal stewardship is an intentional care plan with action steps.

So, here's the question. How do you find the desire to embrace discipline and dedication so making good wellness choices doesn't seem like work?

Perhaps this is the key: *Whatever may be your task, work at it heartily (from the soul), as [something done] for the Lord and not for men* (Colossians 3:23 AMPC). In context, this is talking about how slaves work under their master's authority. But I think we can extrapolate a mindset that is fitting for us as we serve under our heavenly Master. Notice this has to do with our *souls.*

The pursuit of being well in body, soul, and spirit is our personal stewardship. Personal stewardship is an intentional care plan with action steps, keeping in mind these things:

- The body is the temple of God.
- The soul is the invisible part of us we take to heaven when we die.
- The spirit is the part that fellowships with God and grows more like him.

Personal stewardship is a matter of obedience to God and a desire to please and glorify him. Obedience isn't always joyful. But it *brings* joy when we obey—when we choose God over self.

To make wellbeing a priority, there are times we have to say no to other good projects and say yes to ourselves. We can't do all the things and do them well. We're really saying yes to taking care of the resources God has invested in us. My aha! moment last week was, "If I don't take care of *me*, there will be no *we*." In this Bible study, let's see how we can endure when stewardship gets hard.

Heavenly Insights

For you know that when your faith is tested, your endurance has a chance to grow. So let it grow, for when your endurance is fully developed, you will be perfect and complete, needing nothing. (James 1:3–4)

When circumstances get in your way, do you feel like you have an "out" from pursuing what is right? How do you address that?

Instead of an *out*, how about allowing a *time out* from the chaos so you have what it takes to develop endurance?

What is the process that develops endurance?

What is the result of endurance?

God blesses those who patiently endure testing and temptation. Afterward they will receive the crown of life that God has promised to those who love him. (James 1:12)

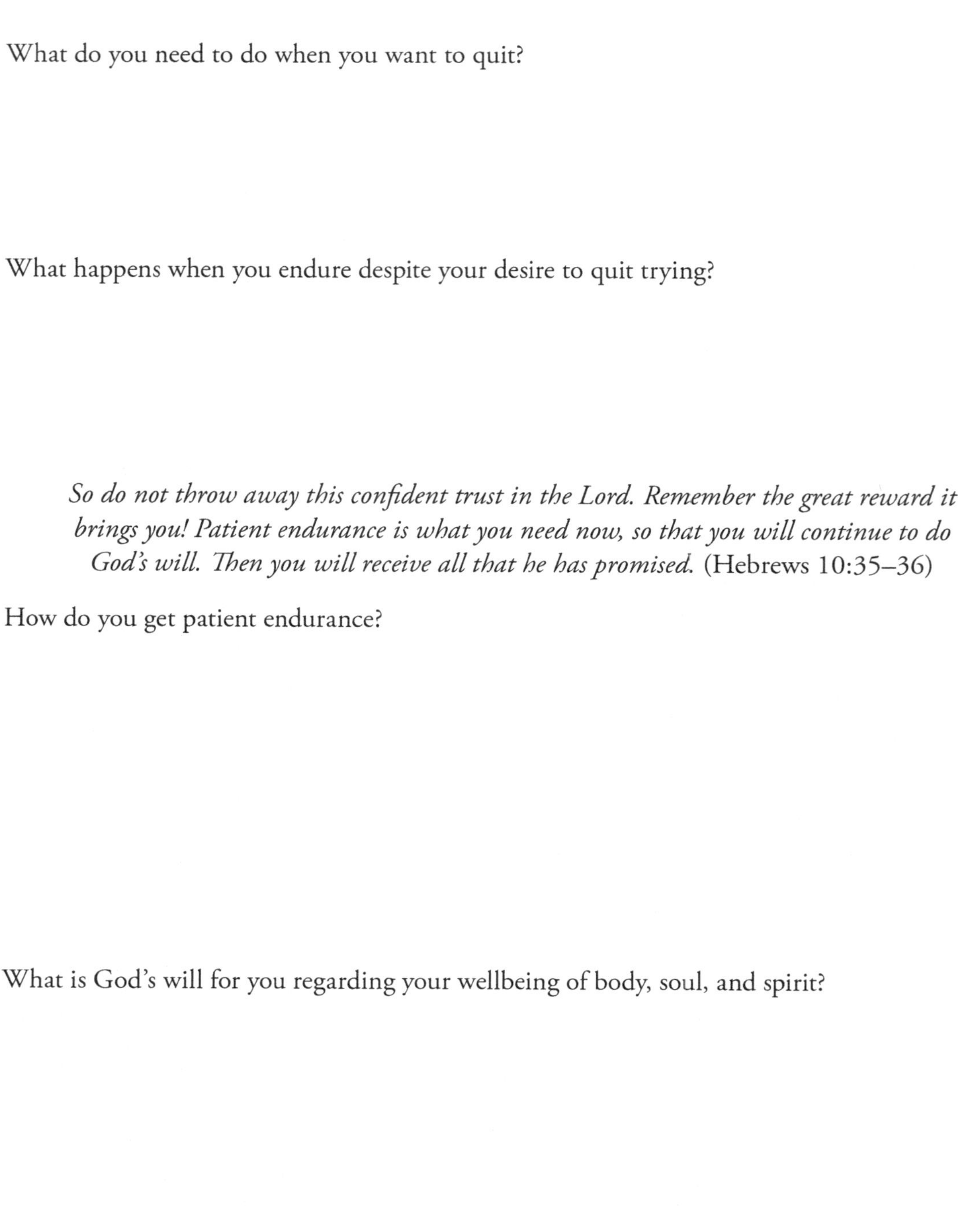

What do you need to do when you want to quit?

What happens when you endure despite your desire to quit trying?

> *So do not throw away this confident trust in the Lord. Remember the great reward it brings you! Patient endurance is what you need now, so that you will continue to do God's will. Then you will receive all that he has promised.* (Hebrews 10:35–36)

How do you get patient endurance?

What is God's will for you regarding your wellbeing of body, soul, and spirit?

> *Yet we hear that some of you are living idle lives, refusing to work and meddling in other people's business. We command such people and urge them in the name of the Lord Jesus Christ to settle down and work to earn their own living. As for the rest of you, dear brothers and sisters, never get tired of doing good.* (2 Thessalonians 3:11–13)

When you apply these same principles to your wellbeing, what are the dangers of being idle in your choices?

What is the danger of complacency?

How do you settle down into a good wellbeing routine?

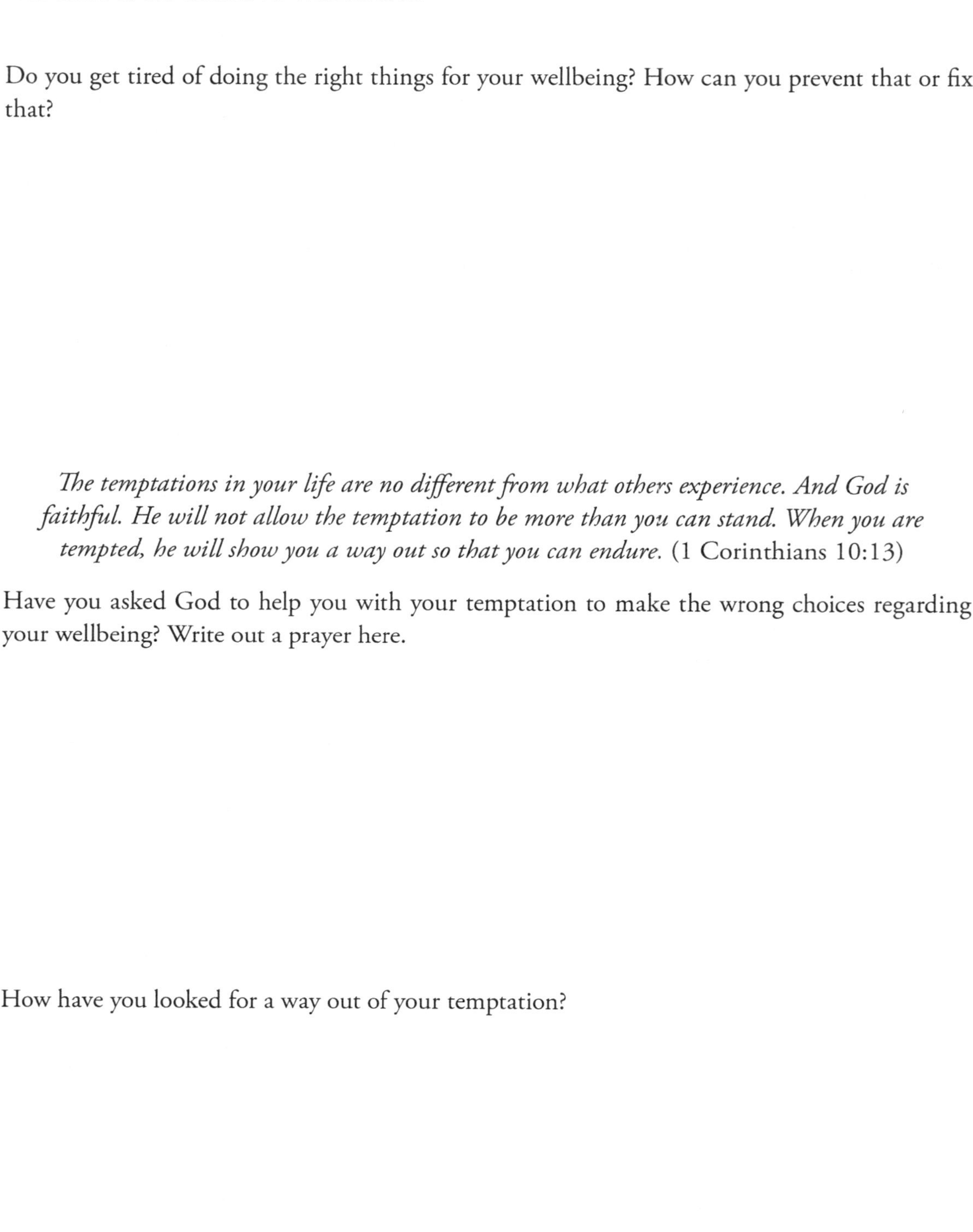

Do you get tired of doing the right things for your wellbeing? How can you prevent that or fix that?

The temptations in your life are no different from what others experience. And God is faithful. He will not allow the temptation to be more than you can stand. When you are tempted, he will show you a way out so that you can endure. (1 Corinthians 10:13)

Have you asked God to help you with your temptation to make the wrong choices regarding your wellbeing? Write out a prayer here.

How have you looked for a way out of your temptation?

Remind yourself how God helped you to endure previously. How can you tap into that again?

Help Me!

Have you made a list of the things you need to do on a consistent basis to be a good steward (take care) of your body? Your soul? Your spirit? Nourishing and nurturing ourselves is not the opposite of being selfless.

First, we have to get rid of some false programming. We've allowed ourselves to be programmed by the unbiblical messages of the world and, yes, even the church. Here are some of the myths that undermine personal stewardship.

- To be successful, you have to be "doing" all the time. Productivity is a measurement of worth.
- To be selfless is to be godly. And to be selfless means you can't take time for yourself.
- When you have a good opportunity, it is an open door from God, and you must go through it to please God.
- You should feel guilty if you take a break. It's laziness, and laziness is not of God.
- Self-care is self-indulgent and puts you first instead of God.
- If you believe you can do it, you can. Just put your mind and effort into it and keep pushing until you make it.
- You deserve to indulge yourself.
- You will have more energy if you eat. Then you can do more without taking a break.

What could you add to that list? How do we de-program and re-program?

- Realize that personal stewardship is an act of worship and obedience to God.
- Rest and refresh before you feel exhausted and burned out. By the time you feel as if you need a break, it's too late to stay on top of things. It's like waiting to be thirsty to drink water. Our bodies need it before they signal a water deficit. Or think of it this way: if we look at our car's fuel gauge, we can safely know we won't run out of gas if we fill it up before we get into the red warning zone.
- Making your list of personal stewardship action steps is not about escaping the demands of your life or rewarding yourself or indulging. It is a care plan that honors God.

Those who live only to satisfy their own sinful nature will harvest decay and death from that sinful nature. But those who live to please the Spirit will harvest everlasting life from the Spirit. So let's not get tired of doing what is good. At just the right time we will reap a harvest of blessing if we don't give up. (Galatians 6:8–9)

- Sometimes, giving in to our circumstances and giving up on our wellbeing intentions leads to the temptation to sin. We take breaks from personal stewardship. What are the possible outcomes and remedies of this?

- The perspective of living to please the Spirit helps us not to get tired of doing what is good. What will you do to prevent giving up?

One little victory for me the last few days is to ask myself, "Are you really hungry?" when I want to grab a snack. It has curbed my actions. I think that's more important than curbing my appetite.

Homework

1. Curb your attitudes. Swap out one myth for one truth regarding personal stewardship.
2. Read "Self-Sabotage" in the resource section.
3. Curb your actions. Based on God's leading, write your wellbeing care plan. (See "Personal Stewardship Care Plan" in the resource section.)
4. What struggles have you had this week? List them and brainstorm ways to prevent or overcome them moving forward.

Health Check

Body: How will I *nourish* my body with food and fitness this week?

Soul: How will I *nurture* my soul with positive relationships this week?

Spirit: How will I *nest* in God's presence during devotion time this week?

If I don't take care of *me*, there will be no *we*.

Hurrahs and Happy Dances

List your victories from the week and celebrate them. Share them with one of your cheerleaders. Note any aha! moments from this week.

Hope Quest

Father, I yield my attitudes and actions to you so I might grow more like you. I am making room in my life for you to do the work you want to do in me. I dedicate my newfound margin to be a good steward of the body, soul, and spirit you created in me. Give me an extra measure of patience in the process and determination to endure when it gets hard.

TRADE SELF-TALK FOR SOUL-TALK

Do you talk to yourself? Some say the older we get, the more we do it. Why is that? Do we lose our filter? Do we give words to our thoughts? Maybe we're just more aware of it. Even before we enter the age of talking to ourselves out loud, we are doing it with our "inside voice."

Often, we create lies that self-sabotage our good intentions, and worse, escalate to self-bullying. It includes thoughts about ourselves and our circumstances. Negative self-talk (our internal voice, not audible words) employs distorted thinking patterns.

In this chapter, we'll look at a different kind of self-talk. Not mumbling any old words. Intentional words we share inside our hearts and minds to reinforce biblical precepts. These words are designed to mature us and minister to our souls.

Heartstrings

The Grin Gal's psalm, inspired by David's soul-talk in Psalms 42 and 43.

> Why am I so overwhelmed? Why do I need to vent so much? Instead, I will focus on God. I will praise him before I even feel like it. God is the one who helps me grin from the inside out. He is my God!

When I am so overwhelmed, I will remind myself of everything I know about my Lord. Scripture is my truth. My life experience is the amen.

When chaos threatens to crash in on my mind, I will remind myself of God's Word. He loves me every minute of every day. During the darkest nights, I will sing songs that help me fix my focus.

If my life is a prayer, what is it saying to God? Do I question him, or do I stand firm on my rock-solid God? When my faith waivers, I will remind myself that my faith isn't in myself but in a God who never fails. When others hurt me and trials afflict me, I will train my focus to look to God.

Why am I so overwhelmed? Why do I need to vent so much? Instead, I will focus on God. I will praise him before I even feel like it. God is the one who helps me grin from the inside out. He is my God!

Why do I keep counting on God when it seems as if he lets me go through hard times? I know his ways are not my ways, and I can't see the bigger picture. Because I know he cares for me, I can wait for a better outcome. This is temporary.

I am trusting God to use his Spirit and his Word like a lantern and compass to guide me through the ups and downs of my life.

I will continue to sing even when it isn't a happy day. We will have a happy heaven, and that's reason enough to bless his name! I worship him with my song, with my words, with my life.

Why am I so overwhelmed? Why do I need to vent so much? Instead, I will focus on God. I will praise him before I even feel like it. God is the one who helps me grin from the inside out. He is my God!

Heavenly Insights

Bless the LORD, O my soul, and all that is within me, bless his holy name! Bless the LORD, O my soul, and forget not all his benefits. (Psalm 103:1–2 ESV)

Any time you read "O my soul" in Scripture, it is a form of soul-talk.

What does the psalmist tell himself here?

What happens when you use those words?

"So commit yourselves wholeheartedly to these words of mine. Tie them to your hands and wear them on your forehead as reminders. Teach them to your children. Talk about them when you are at home and when you are on the road, when you are going to bed and when you are getting up." (Deuteronomy 11:18–19)

How do you adhere God's Word to your soul?

Replace humanistic self-talk with biblical soul-talk by keeping God's words close by.

Set your mind and keep focused habitually on the things above [the heavenly things], not on things that are on the earth [which have only temporal value]. (Colossians 3:2 AMP)

Choose soul-talk that is healthy and biblical.

How do you keep a proper focus through soul-talk?

How do you create a soul-talk habit?

> *And now, dear brothers and sisters, one final thing. Fix your thoughts on what is true, and honorable, and right, and pure, and lovely, and admirable. Think about things that are excellent and worthy of praise.* (Philippians 4:8)

How do you fix your thoughts?

Give an example for how to line up your soul-talk to make sure what you say to yourself fits with the values mentioned in this verse.

We've looked at this verse before. Let's look at it in the AMPC:

> *Do not be conformed to this world (this age), [fashioned after and adapted to its external, superficial customs], but be transformed (changed) by the [entire] renewal of your mind [by its new ideals and its new attitude], so that you may prove [for yourselves] what is the good and acceptable and perfect will of God, even the thing which is good and acceptable and perfect [in His sight for you].* (Romans 12:2 AMPC)

Soul-talk desires for God to be center stage and self to be a supporting actress.

Help Me!

Learning positive self-talk might be dangerous if it increases your focus on self. It can be self-centered and humanistic. Some techniques encourage you to lie to yourself to create a fake reality. It isn't possible to create a better reality by simply declaring it.

How do you know you're on track for biblical soul-talk and not humanistic self-talk? One way is to evaluate your motivation. The motives we aim for:

- God's glory.
- Spiritual health of the soul.

Examples of negative self-talk

- I will never succeed at healthy eating because I'm a failure.
- I'll never change.
- I can't bear this current circumstance.
- There's no solution to this problem.
- If God really cared, he would help me. He must not love me.

Counter with soul-talk

- I can do this as God leads because he will help me. God is not a failure. I will do this in his power and for his glory.
- God is changing me—transformed to fulfill his purpose.
- God is equipping me to endure this circumstance. And he is bearing my burden for me.
- God will lead me to know what I need to do. He doesn't leave me hanging with no answers. He will help me either escape the problem or to cope with it if it doesn't change.
- God does care. He is available to help me. He loves me so much that he won't leave me alone to handle this.

Steps to biblical soul-talk

Your soul already talks to itself. This isn't about adding in self-talk. It's about changing from unhealthy self-talk to God-honoring soul-talk.

1. **Clear the noise.** Before you can do the rest of these steps, you have to quiet the busy and calm the calamity. Give the quiet voice inside enough silence and space so it can speak out. Before we can have soul-talk, we need to have self-hush!
2. **Listen to your current self-talk.** Identify any lies. Evaluate if you have self-bullying tendencies.
3. **Heed the Holy Spirit.** Ask him to show your sinful ways and thoughts. Confess them to God. By clearing the clutter of sin away, you have a blank space to fill. The Holy Spirit doesn't only convict of sin, though. He is also the Comforter. We need him in all his roles as we work through biblical soul-talk.
4. **Shift your focus.** Self-talk fixates on self. (That's stating the obvious, isn't it?) Soul-talk desires for God to be center stage and self to be a supporting actress.
5. **Pray for discernment.** Ask God to show you the truth about yourself. This is not about living "your own truth" but about living God's truth about you.
6. **Take on God's view of you.** This new perspective might surprise you!
7. **Implement new words.** When you catch yourself stating unbiblical self-talk, switch it for life-affirming words from Scripture. Personalize it. Don't just eradicate negative thinking. Instead, be intentional about biblical soul-talk on a regular basis.

Homework

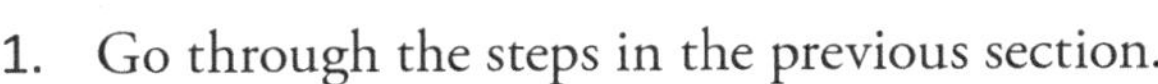

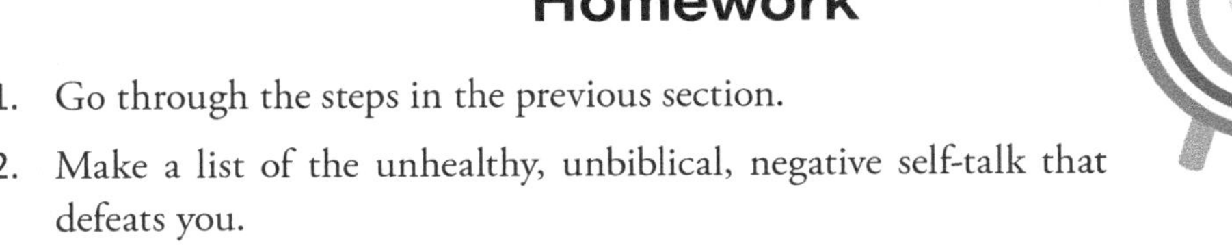

1. Go through the steps in the previous section.
2. Make a list of the unhealthy, unbiblical, negative self-talk that defeats you.

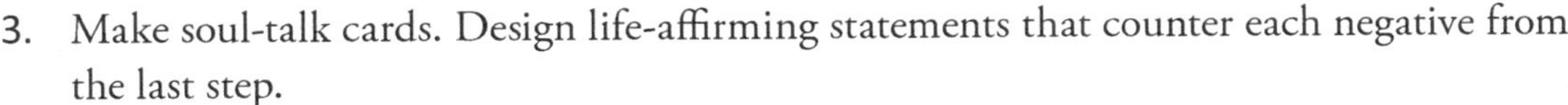

3. Make soul-talk cards. Design life-affirming statements that counter each negative from the last step.
4. What struggles have you had this week? List them and brainstorm ways to prevent or overcome them moving forward.

Health Check

Body: How am I doing with identifying self-sabotage regarding my food and fitness plan?

Soul: How has my soul-talk changed this week?

Spirit: Did I consult the Holy Spirit to inform my thoughts and feelings this week?

Take on God's view of you.

Hurrahs and Happy Dances

List your victories from the week and celebrate them. Share them with one of your cheerleaders. Note any aha! moments from this week.

Hope Quest

Papa God, I can't fathom your love for me, but I receive it. I don't always counter my unhealthy self-talk with soul-talk from your Word, but that is what I desire. Help me resist self-bullying and embrace your comfort. Show me the lies I tell myself and help me evict them. Fill the vacancy with your truth.

GETTING STRONGER

I started working out in the football players' weight room during my senior year of high school. This alone is laughable, considering I wasn't an athlete and truthfully didn't even get the "easy A" in gym class. As a young adult, I joined the Y, where a professional bodybuilder trained me. How strong could I become?

I learned how to "lift to failure." Rather than doing more repetitions at an easy weight, you do full range of motion reps with a heavy weight until your muscle quivers and fails to do the lift. Then you know you have maxed out your muscle's potential.

Even today, I love gaining strength. Not just physical muscles—I'm growing my spiritual muscles too. Every once in a while, I'll test my muscles to failure. And every once in a while, life tests my soul to failure too. The more I build up my God muscles, the more I can handle those life tests.

If you fail under pressure, your strength is too small. (Proverbs 24:10)

Heartstrings

A popular artist sings, "What doesn't kill you makes you stronger." Sometimes when I'm going through tough stuff, I sing that line to myself. Maybe you've caught yourself doing the same thing. But after reading Scripture and thinking about times when I didn't grow from an experience, I started to rethink the concept.

I looked up the background and discovered the quote was first coined by German philosopher Friedrich Nietzsche.[9] To decide if this is true wisdom, we have to check it with the truth of the Bible and also the truth of Christian experience.

Here's what I've learned from studying this:

- When we go through difficult experiences, we have a choice if we will merely get through it or if we will grow from it. Sometimes we learn. Sometimes we lean. Sometimes we lose.
- We have the opportunity to go through trials alone or choose to welcome God's presence to strengthen us and his people to support us.
- Some trials leave us feeling wounded, battle weary, and empty. What do we do with that?

What I eventually realized is that strength comes from the inside out, and the source of unfailing strength comes from the Lord. Other kinds of strength don't have the staying power God's strength gives me.

Build up your God muscles. No spinach required—just faith! Today's heavenly insights show us how we can be strengthened—it isn't through a struggle; it's through a Savior. Plug into God's strength to prevent power outages.

Heavenly Insights

I thank Christ Jesus our Lord, who has given me strength to do his work. He considered me trustworthy and appointed me to serve him. (1 Timothy 1:12)

Why does Jesus give Paul, the writer of this passage, strength?

What qualified Paul for this, according to the second sentence?

Do you think Jesus will strengthen you to do his work too? If so, how does this passage inspire you with renewed actions or attitudes?

It isn't through a struggle, it's through a Savior.

I am dying from grief; my years are shortened by sadness. Sin has drained my strength; I am wasting away from within. (Psalm 31:10)

How do sadness and grief affect your wellbeing?

How does sin affect your strength?

Have you ever felt as if you were dying from the inside out? Describe that.

He gives power to the weak and strength to the powerless. (Isaiah 40:29)

God doesn't say he gives power to the powerless and strength to the weak. Since this passage doesn't state the obvious, it makes me want to dig in and pay attention!

What do strength and power do for you when you feel you have none?

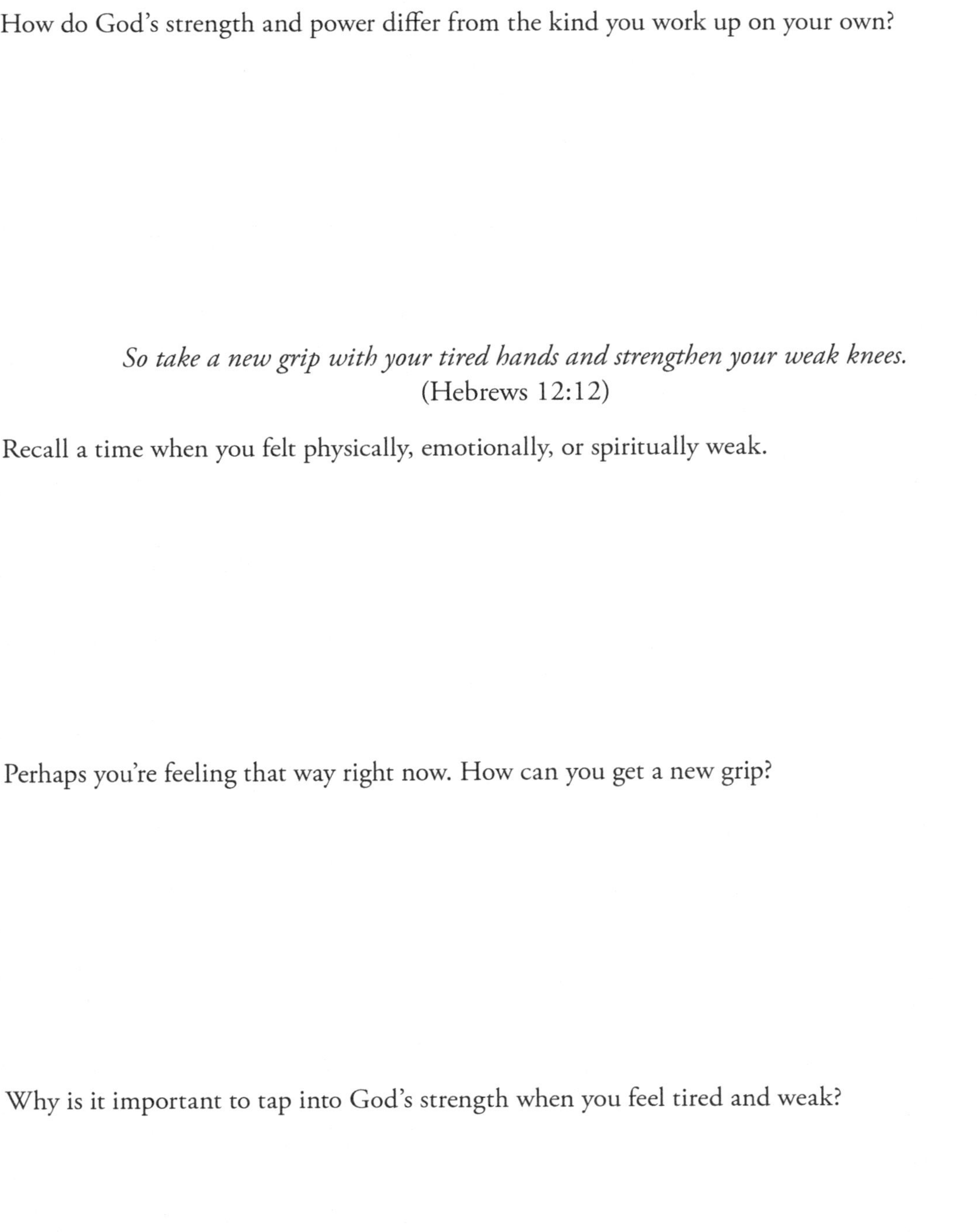

How do God's strength and power differ from the kind you work up on your own?

So take a new grip with your tired hands and strengthen your weak knees.
(Hebrews 12:12)

Recall a time when you felt physically, emotionally, or spiritually weak.

Perhaps you're feeling that way right now. How can you get a new grip?

Why is it important to tap into God's strength when you feel tired and weak?

Even there your hand will guide me, and your strength will support me.
(Psalm 139:10)

Read all of Psalm 139 for the context. *There* reflects a list of places David might go, but he can never escape from God's Spirit. We can never isolate ourselves from God. How does God's hand guide you when you think you are away from his presence?

When was the last time you didn't deserve God's strength, but he supported you anyway? What a good reminder of the enormity of God's love for us!

You are their glorious strength. It pleases you to make us strong. (Psalm 89:17)

What is the adjective to the word strength here? What does that mean to you?

What pleases God, according to the second sentence?

Let's spend time getting strengthened by God since we know it pleases him. It isn't just any ol' strength. It's *glorious* strength!

Extra reading:

- Psalm 18:1, 32
- Psalm 22:19
- Psalm 28:7
- Psalm 29:11
- Psalm 46:1
- Psalm 68:35
- Psalm 73:26
- Psalm 138:3
- Isaiah 58:10–11
- Philippians 4:13
- 2 Thessalonians 3:3

Plug into God's strength to prevent power outages.

Help Me!

To get to a place of strength in body, soul, and spirit, we have some work to do! Here are some ideas to help you on your way.

Reword this prayer as if someone were praying over you. *I pray that from his glorious, unlimited resources he will empower you with inner strength through his Spirit* (Ephesians 3:16).

Write out the following verse on a card or sticky note as a reminder. Try to memorize it. *"The Lord is my strength and my song; he has given me victory. This is my God, and I will praise him—my father's God, and I will exalt him!"* (Exodus 15:2).

Think about your life. How has God been your strength and protection?

How has God rewritten your story?

Consider telling someone else about it as a way of giving testimony to his goodness but also as a reminder of where you get your strength. *My life is an example to many, because you have been my strength and protection* (Psalm 71:7).

Build up your God muscles

1. **Seek God-strength rather than self-strength.** *Search for the LORD and for his strength; continually seek him* (1 Chronicles 16:11 and Psalm 105:4).
2. **Full-on commit to God—with nothing held back.** *"The eyes of the LORD search the whole earth in order to strengthen those whose hearts are fully committed to him. What a fool you have been! From now on you will be at war"* (2 Chronicles 16:9).
3. **Receive God's strength renewal often (or, as we say, rinse and repeat**). *He renews my strength. He guides me along right paths, bringing honor to his name* (Psalm 23:3).
4. **Wait.** Make sure you sense God as close in the waiting times as in the going times. *You are my strength; I wait for you to rescue me, for you, O God, are my fortress* (Psalm 59:9).
5. **Trust.** Lean into your Papa God. He is reliable. He wants what is best for you based on a kingdom perspective. *"See, God has come to save me. I will trust in him and not be afraid. The LORD GOD is my strength and my song; he has given me victory"* (Isaiah 12:2).
6. **Get strong.** Seek God as the source of your strength. Tap into him and let him pump you up. *The people will declare, "The LORD is the source of all my righteousness and strength"* (Isaiah 45:24).
7. **Leave it all to God.** *"But my work seems so useless! I have spent my strength for nothing and to no purpose. Yet I leave it all in the LORD's hand; I will trust God for my reward"* (Isaiah 49:4).
8. **Put your inner grin on!** *A cheerful heart is good medicine, but a broken spirit saps a person's strength* (Proverbs 17:22).
9. **Remember where your strength comes from.** *I look up to the mountains; does my strength come from mountains? No, my strength comes from GOD, who made heaven, and earth, and mountains* (Psalm 121:1–2 MSG).

Homework

1. Pick some of the Bible verses from this chapter and print them out in a way that will impact you in your strength-training routine of body, soul, and spirit.
2. Read "Strength Training" and "Back to the Gym" in the resource section if you haven't already.
3. Journal about any perceived weaknesses that you think are holding you back from reaching your full potential in Christ.
4. What struggles have you had this week? List them and brainstorm ways to prevent or overcome them moving forward.

Health Check

Body: What am I doing to incorporate a strength-training component into my fitness routine?

Soul: What is my weakness? How is God turning it into a strength?

Spirit: Do I lean into God with a posture of trust when I feel weak?

Hurrahs and Happy Dances

List your victories from the week and celebrate them. Share them with one of your cheerleaders. Note any aha! moments from this week.

Hope Quest

This prayer is inspired by 2 Thessalonians 2:16–17.

Father, Son, and Holy Spirit, I receive comfort from your love and grace. When I think of how your love reached out and surprised me, I'm touched by the help and confidence you bring my way. Strengthen me in body, soul, and spirit. As you plant in my life a fresh heart, it invigorates me with wonderful hope. May everything I do and say reflect you more.

SIDETRACKED

The struggle of being sidetracked is something we all deal with! Proverbs 4:27 says, *Don't get sidetracked; keep your feet from following evil.* We think of evil as the "bad" sins, but we need to evaluate anything that keeps us from God's best for our lives. Where we point our feet and our focus helps us not get sidetracked.

It's easy to get sidetracked, "slidetracked" (my made-up word for sliding backward away from our goals), or distracted. The key to deal with it is to identify what your priorities are based on God's Word and how his Spirit leads in your life—everything else is secondary. Why is it we tend to give the wrong things our best focus and energy, cutting short the time we can address what really matters? That's pretty common with humanity in general and with me in particular!

Heartstrings

When I was in Bible college, Mrs. Norma Gillming equipped women for the ministry life. She taught through an organizational system called SHE: Sidetracked Home Executives™. We created files to organize daily, weekly, monthly, and seasonal tasks. Oh, if life were only that simple!

But the truth is, life is full of distractions. We easily get sidetracked by whatever grabs our attention. Not only do we chase after things that have less value, but we procrastinate addressing the primary focus that God *does* have in our lives.

Friends shared their answers to the following questions:

What are some things that cause you to get sidetracked from your wellbeing goals?

- **Working.** I'm a workaholic and have a hard time stopping enough to tend to my personal wellbeing.
- **Laziness.** I just don't have the "want to" it takes. My energy and mental focus are shot.
- **Busyness.** I'm overcommitted as it is and just can't add one more thing, even if it means sacrificing my own wellbeing.
- **Poor planning.** I'm really disorganized when it comes to making wellbeing a priority. Making plans seems like work.

What wellbeing intentions get overlooked due to being sidetracked?

- **Stretching and exercise.** I don't stop my other projects to do my stretches or exercise videos. If I don't make them a priority, they don't happen.
- **Water intake.** I know it's good for me, but I can't seem to do it.
- **Rest.** Even when I set aside time to rest and refresh, I have a hard time relaxing. And getting restorative sleep seems impossible.
- **Meal planning.** When I'm on the other side of a meal-planned week, I'm grateful for how easy it is to put meals together. But gathering recipes, planning meals, and making a grocery list is so time-consuming!

Distractions take me away from the best wellbeing practices. I need to make a special effort to stay vigilant about my sidetracked tendencies and pray for a narrow focus. Hey, I know! I'm going to let myself get sidetracked by the things that are good for me instead of the things that take me further from wellbeing!

Where we point our feet and our focus helps us not get sidetracked.

Heavenly Insights

Then Jesus said, "Let's go off by ourselves to a quiet place and rest awhile." He said this because there were so many people coming and going that Jesus and his apostles didn't even have time to eat. (Mark 6:31)

What do you see Jesus teaching the apostles to help with the pressures from other people?

Have you ever given yourself a timeout when life gets too stressful or you feel too scattered? How does that help you focus on the main thing?

Jesus prescribed a quiet place and rest. Does that come easy to you? Do you crave it? Do you make it a point to get it despite how busy you are?

The apostles didn't even have time to eat. Yet Jesus showed them how to make time. That shows it's important to take care of yourself. When others demand so much of your time and energy, don't neglect your personal needs.

> *Don't waste your time on useless work, mere busywork, the barren pursuits of darkness. Expose these things for the sham they are. It's a scandal when people waste their lives on things they must do in the darkness where no one will see. Rip the cover off those frauds and see how attractive they look in the light of Christ. Wake up from your sleep, Climb out of your coffins; Christ will show you the light! So watch your step. Use your head. Make the most of every chance you get. These are desperate times!* (Ephesians 5:11–16 MSG)

What is sidetracking you from what God wants you to do?

Do you ever feel as if what you are doing is a waste? Write about that here.

How can you make the most of every opportunity you get?

Do you procrastinate addressing the primary focus God has in your life?

You were running the race so well. Who has held you back from following the truth? It certainly isn't God, for he is the one who called you to freedom. (Galatians 5:7–8)

Can you relate to this statement? "I was doing so well with my wellbeing journey. But then fill-in-the-blank started to hold me back from making progress. I don't know how to get back on track."

What do you think God would have you do to avoid getting sidetracked or to remedy it when it happens?

Help Me!

Getting sidetracked isn't merely a current culture dilemma. In Bible times, Christ-followers lost focus too. I think of Peter walking on the water toward Jesus. When he took his eyes off the Lord and noticed the circumstances around him, he started to sink. That's how I feel when I get sidetracked too—*I'm sinking, I'm sinking!*

I also think of how Martha got distracted by doing all the chores of entertaining company and missed the most important thing—being at Jesus's feet like Mary. I want to be like Mary, but I'm wired more like Martha! How many days do I let the chores of the day distract me from the delights of the moment?

In Galatians 1:10, we are warned about the distraction of being people pleasers. *Obviously, I'm not trying to win the approval of people, but of God. If pleasing people were my goal, I would not be Christ's servant.* Whose approval are you trying to win? It's hard to resist! I don't like to let people down. I have to reverse out of that way of thinking and realize the real prize goes to the one who wants to please God alone.

Tips to avoid being sidetracked

1. **Fix your focus on God's lead.** Let your eyes look right on [with fixed purpose], and let your gaze be straight before you (Proverbs 4:25 AMPC).
2. **Pray for God's help when stressed.** Please listen and answer me, for I am overwhelmed by my troubles (Psalm 55:2).
3. **Make it a priority to have quiet time with God.** Before daybreak the next morning, Jesus got up and went out to an isolated place to pray (Mark 1:35).

Ways to prevent being sidetracked from wellbeing priorities

1. **Accountability.** Tell a friend your wellbeing plan and ask her to hold you to it. Decide in advance how many details to share. Create a plan that involves a balance of next steps for wellbeing that includes care of the body, soul, and spirit.
2. **Easy-access exercise.** Set it up so all you have to do is show up and do the work. Get dressed in workout clothes when you get up in the morning so you're ready to go when it's time.

3. **Checklists and habit trackers.** You will do your best when you have a specific plan. Some are motivated by tracking lists and checking off accomplishments. If you respond to rewards, give yourself a reward for a completed monthly chart. Make it something that supports your wellbeing goals rather than derails them.

Homework

1. Choose one plan at a time and dive in. Select from: meal planner, food tracker, fitness plan, habit tracker, etc.
2. Keep your priorities in front of you. Have a motivational/inspirational vision board or journal.
3. What struggles have you had this week? List them and brainstorm ways to prevent or overcome them moving forward.

Health Check

Body: Why am I getting sidetracked from my goals for physical wellbeing?

Soul: How is my soul affected when I get sidetracked?

Spirit: When I'm sidetracked, how will my spirit commune with God and get me back on track?

Hurrahs and Happy Dances

List your victories from the week and celebrate them. Share them with one of your cheerleaders. Note any aha! moments from this week.

Hope Quest

O Father, the one who keeps me focused on the goal.

Put blinders on me to limit the distractions.

Give me a will to resist the temptations of pleasing others.

And help the stresses of this world not to
hold me back from pleasing you.

Show me how wellbeing is as important in my life as Jesus made it to be.

SOUL GOALS

What can you do to take care of your soul? Soul goals help that inner being we can't see but defines who we are—our unique identity. The mind, heart, and personality. We put so much effort into physical achievements and spiritual focus, but we need to take care of our souls, as well. In this chapter, we'll look at being a good caregiver of our souls.

My husband is a hospice chaplain, and one thing he has noticed is that when the physical is almost gone, the soul can still thrive—but it takes a little maintenance. The patients who have tended to the invisible part of their beings are better able to cope with setbacks and adjust to the idea of having a terminal diagnosis. At the same time they anticipate heaven, they also make every day count here on earth. We don't need to be dying to do that—how can we start now?

Heartstrings

How can we make our souls a higher priority in our lives? And if we did emphasize soul care, how would we know if our attempts have been successful? I've been revamping the way I think about success lately. Here's one example of that. The Life, Repurposed Facebook group I'm a part of wanted to celebrate goals we've achieved lately. Michelle Rayburn, the leader, asked us to report in. I've been setting goals since I was fourteen and have been labeled an overachiever. So, you would think my response to this goal celebration request would be to tell them of a book release or a client success or some other achievement. Instead, this is what I posted:

> I'm thinking of some post-COVID re-entry goals. They were my anticipation for fifteen months. Getting my hair cut. Going to church. Joining a gym. Eating at a restaurant. Spending time with friends. Going shopping. All such simple things, but after that long of a wait, it seemed like achieving big goals! And yes, not much work on my part, but sometimes, the work that takes place in our souls is as important as productivity that can be measured by success.

Michelle responded, "Soul goals!"[10]

And that's what I want to encourage us to have here. Soul goals. We set physical goals such as weighing a certain amount or having a fitness plan, but what are we doing for our souls?

Heavenly Insights

"I am leaving you with a gift—peace of mind and heart. And the peace I give is a gift the world cannot give. So don't be troubled or afraid." (John 14:27)

Peace goes a long way toward soul health, doesn't it? What does this verse tell you about peace?

How does being troubled or afraid mess up your peace?

How can you deal with those two specific challenges?

What needs to change to have more moments of peace?

> *Those who are dominated by the sinful nature think about sinful things, but those who are controlled by the Holy Spirit think about things that please the Spirit. So letting your sinful nature control your mind leads to death. But letting the Spirit control your mind leads to life and peace.* (Romans 8:5–6)

The book of Romans shows us that the battle of sin and rebellion against God begins in the mind. How do you make a conscious effort not to think about sinful things?

How do you let the Holy Spirit control you? When you do this, how does this affect your thought life?

What leads to death?

What leads to life and peace?

The work that takes place in our souls is as important as measurable productivity.

But there is another power within me that is at war with my mind. This power makes me a slave to the sin that is still within me. Oh, what a miserable person I am! Who will free me from this life that is dominated by sin and death? Thank God! The answer is in Jesus Christ our Lord. So you see how it is: In my mind I really want to obey God's law, but because of my sinful nature I am a slave to sin. (Romans 7:23–25)

We all recognize the tug-of-war between good intentions and sinful nature. Right before this passage in Romans, we hear the writer, Paul, say he doesn't do what he wants to do (please God) and ends up doing what he doesn't want to do (sinning).

Thankfully, Paul doesn't leave us hanging in this epistle, and neither does God! It says clearly about our dilemma: *The answer is in Jesus Christ our Lord.*

How does Jesus make the difference in your thought life?

How does your thought life influence your actions?

Consider the other role of Jesus in this passage—*Lord*. Making him Lord is much more than Savior. What does it mean to you?

So prepare your minds for action and exercise self-control. Put all your hope in the gracious salvation that will come to you when Jesus Christ is revealed to the world. (1 Peter 1:13)

It's obvious that preparing our minds helps us have God-pleasing actions. How does a person exercise self-control?

How does that help prepare your mind?

Help Me!

When was the last day you recall having a peaceful mind and heart during all your waking hours? Describe it.

> *Don't worry about anything; instead, pray about everything. Tell God what you need, and thank him for all he has done. Then you will experience God's peace, which exceeds anything we can understand. His peace will guard your hearts and minds as you live in Christ Jesus.* (Philippians 4:6–7)

The Message paraphrase words it this way:

> *Don't fret or worry. Instead of worrying, pray. Let petitions and praises shape your worries into prayers, letting God know your concerns. Before you know it, a sense of God's wholeness, everything coming together for good, will come and settle you down. It's wonderful what happens when Christ displaces worry at the center of your life.*

What tips to take care of our souls come through as you read this? Here's what I see:

1. Address any fear or worry issues. Don't let them stew.
2. Replace worry with prayer. (I know some smoking-cessation techniques that involve snapping a rubber band around your wrist. Maybe our Spirit-led behavior modification involves stopping to pray when we detect our minds going away from faith into doubt.)
3. Tell God your petitions, letting God know what concerns you.
4. While taking a pitstop to manage worry, take time to praise God.
5. Focus on sensing God's wholeness and peace. Allow his Spirit to "settle you down."

Take a moment right now to write a prayer in this journal space, using Philippians 4:6–7 as your pattern. Make sure to do this with your soul wide awake, taking care of your heart and mind.

We studied John 14:27 in our last section. Look how the Amplified Bible Classic Edition words this verse. (The AMPC is basically a traditional Bible version plus a Bible dictionary.)

> *Peace I leave with you; My [own] peace I now give and bequeath to you. Not as the world gives do I give to you. Do not let your hearts be troubled, neither let them be afraid. [Stop allowing yourselves to be agitated and disturbed; and do not permit yourselves to be fearful and intimidated and cowardly and unsettled.]*

Now read it in *The Message* paraphrase:

> *"I'm telling you these things while I'm still living with you. The Friend, the Holy Spirit whom the Father will send at my request, will make everything plain to you. He will remind you of all the things I have told you. I'm leaving you well and whole. That's my parting gift to you. Peace. I don't leave you the way you're used to being left—feeling abandoned, bereft. So don't be upset. Don't be distraught."*

Notice how each version expands our perspective on this passage. Journal what stands out to you. This will help you deal with what threatens to rob your peace.

Focus verse:

> *Devote yourselves to prayer with an alert mind and a thankful heart.* (Colossians 4:2)

Homework

1. Spend some time journaling your thoughts by processing the verses and tips from this chapter.
2. When you're trying to lasso your thoughts into better control, ask yourself, "Does this thought please the Spirit?"
3. Set aside some time to take care of your soul. What are your soul goals?

4. What struggles have you had this week? List them and brainstorm ways to prevent or overcome them moving forward.

Health Check

Body: How am I creating a peaceful environment?

Soul: Did I set aside intentional, dedicated time this week to take care of my soul?

Spirit: Am I making Jesus Lord of my life with my thoughts and actions, or am I going rogue?

When was the last day you recall having a peaceful mind and heart during all your waking hours?

Hurrahs and Happy Dances

List your victories from the week and celebrate them. Share them with one of your cheerleaders. Note any aha! moments from this week.

Hope Quest

Father, today I'm setting my intentions on taking care of my soul. Help me with my thought life. May the words I speak in my mind and the emotions dwelling in my heart please you.

Resources

EATING HEALTHY ON A BUDGET

One of the biggest complaints I get about trying to eat healthy is that it's too expensive. I have several views on that. Some ingredients cost more money than you are used to spending. But because you are eating out less, eating fewer processed foods, and eating smaller portions, it should even out for your budget. Just don't have sticker shock on a few of the products you now want to stock up on! In this resource chapter, you will find tips on meal planning, meal prep, and saving money.

Meal planning

For meal planning, I use a combination of sources (including cookbooks, online recipes saved to Pinterest, and my own go-to recipes). My process is:

1. Organize my menu the week before. Keep in mind what I have on hand that I need to use up, plus what I need to stock up on (can look at sales ads). I plan some bulk meals to freeze and also ways to use up leftovers and ingredients so there is minimal waste. I prepare ahead for days I need easy options since I cook every meal. One priority is to plan menus that use up the fresh produce earlier in the week so it doesn't spoil.
2. Make a grocery list from step one. I do this online and order curbside pick-up for Saturday morning.
3. On the weekend, I do meal prep. I also make some baked goods to put in the freezer.
4. During the week, I cook lunch and dinner every single day. Meals are for Mom (who lives with us), Hubby, and me. Some are easy, and some are more complex.
5. My aim is for at least one new recipe per week, some recipes from my resources that I've made before, and some meals that I can cook from memory.

Ways to make it easier

- Make a large batch of soup once or twice a week and freeze into meal-sized containers.

- Boil five pounds of ground beef to cook fast, drain, then divide into meal-sized portions in resealable freezer bags. If you prefer your hamburger browned, you can always add it to a skillet to brown it after it has been boiled.
- Partially thaw quite a few chicken breasts or chicken tenderloins so they are still stiff but you're able to cut through them. (Easier than when completely thawed.) Cut into cube-sized bites. Add raw cubes with one cup of chicken broth (I use Better Than Bouillon brand, one teaspoon in one cup boiling water.) Add to Instant Pot and cook for five minutes. Release. Save the broth for another recipe and portion out the cubed chicken breast into meal-sized quantities in resealable bags. (If you don't have an Instant Pot, you can do this on top of the stove in a saucepan.)
- Plan a salad meal. Or make Mason jar salads for several lunches. (Can turn cooked hamburger into taco meat for a taco salad or cooked cubed chicken breasts for a salad protein.) Other salad options: cheeseburger salad, chef salad, or grilled chicken with apples, pecans, and salad greens. Don't forget, beans and peas of various kinds work great in salads! (Garbanzo, black, kidney, edamame, etc.)
- One quick menu includes a grilled protein, a low-carb veggie, and a starchy veggie, along with a fruit salad that can double as dessert.

More tips

If you boil your ground beef in water to cook it in bulk, what do you do with that water and fat you drained off? I throw the boiled water outdoors and not down my drain. That does a great job of getting rid of the fat in a safe way. If you can't throw it outdoors, put a paper towel into a strainer and pour the fatty water through, and it will catch a lot of it. And if you add Dawn dish detergent to the remaining water going down the drain, it helps the fat not accumulate as much. But the best way is for it not to go down the drain!

Buy fresh produce when in season if possible. It is more affordable, sourced closer to home, and tastes better. During off-seasons, you can still get the same product, but it might come from farther away. When that happens, they often harvest it before it's at the best stage. During shipping and storage, it loses some freshness.

Support your local farmers' market for the freshest produce. Yes, this sometimes costs more. But you might be satisfied to eat less of it since it is more flavorful than some grocery store produce. Or it is so amazing you can get by without eating meat with that meal—a big savings. I have always wanted to get a co-op box of produce, either delivered to me weekly or available for pickup. Unfortunately, I don't live in a service area. Here's a good resource to see if you do: www.localharvest.org/csa

One of the struggles for healthy cooking and baking is buying pricey ingredients and then never needing them again. Consider using what you have on hand by choosing a swap. In the chart below, if you see an ingredient the recipe calls for that you don't have, look along the same row and see if you have a possible substitution. This will help you eat healthy on a budget. Be brave and experiment. Some of my best recipes started because I didn't have an ingredient and had to come up with a workaround.

Lime, lemon
Fresh oranges, mandarins, clementines, canned mandarin oranges
Sour cream, yogurt, cottage cheese liquified in the blender, cream cheese
Mashed bananas, applesauce, mashed avocado, blended pineapple
Sometimes different types of flour are interchangeable, depending on your dietary preferences. Get to know your ingredients to understand not all are a 1:1 ratio when swapping. Almond flour, chickpea flour, coconut flour, oat flour (often milled in my kitchen from old-fashioned rolled oats), white wheat flour, etc.
Ground meat of any kind (beef, chicken, turkey, lean pork, chopped meat from leftovers, sausage)
Flax seeds, chia seeds, sesame seeds, hemp hearts

You can save money on harder-to-find items by ordering them online. I use www.vitacost.com and www.amazon.com.

Prepping produce

How do you deal with produce so it doesn't spoil and is ready to go? I rinse produce in a clean sink filled with water and several splashes of white vinegar. This is great for berries. When I make trips to the farmer's market, that produce is more expensive, and I want to make sure it doesn't spoil before I can use it! Once it sits in the vinegar water for a bit, I rinse it off, set it on the counter lined with dish towels to air dry, then put it in storage bags with paper towels to absorb any extra moisture. (Some food preppers disagree with this method, so your mileage may vary.)

One of our Wellbeing Warriors from the focus group added to this idea. Kathy Perrine wrote, "I prep produce using a similar method. I use a spray bottle with half water and half vinegar. Let sprayed produce sit briefly. Then rinse and drain as suggested above to get the produce as dry as possible before storing or freezing. Perhaps I don't buy as much at a time, so this works for smaller amounts."

More tips from readers

When using chicken as an option, large packages of chicken thighs and breasts are generally much cheaper—especially bone-in chicken thighs. I often bring the meat home and weigh and split it up for my recipes before freezing. The same can be true of ground beef. (Tammy Anderud)

I eat from the inventory. Every few weeks, I take inventory of the pantry, fridge, and freezer. I plan meals around what I have on hand and only have to buy fresh fruits and veggies. (Edna Earney)

For me, meal planning is the goal. If I'm using half a cucumber in one recipe, I meal plan to use the other half of the cucumber in the week. This makes my veggie budget more affordable. (Edna Earney)

We buy meat on sale and portion it out for just the two of us. Canned goods, etc. on sale. Most weeks, all we need to buy is bread, milk, and fresh produce. (Melinda Morton)

Shop the ads. I always look for what is on sale and then plan my menu rather than the other way around. (Mary Pielenz Hampton)

I go to the reduced-meat section of my store and get things to throw in the freezer. They usually become part of next week's menu. (Stephenie Hovland)

Drinking lots of water before you eat cuts down on the amount you eat. Plan a menu for each week and shop *only* for what's on the menu. (Janet Pierce)

Ever since COVID, I have shopped for almost all my groceries online. There is no delivery charge over $35, and I save so much money by not being in a store and adding all kinds of extra stuff to my cart. (Letitia Suk)

I try to use foods for several meals in a week. For instance, I will make a pork roast and serve with rice/gravy and veggies of choice. Next day, mix some barbecue sauce with the pork and make sliders. Another day in the week, I use it to make taquitos. I make the leftover rice into a Mexican rice dish. Top baked veggies with meat for an even healthier version. (Carmen Walker)

Here's an example of how to stretch chicken into additional meals. One night, make broiled chicken with veggies. The next night, chicken/veggie quesadillas. If I have more left, I use it to top baked potatoes. (Nancy Graves)

I shop sales and keep an inventory. If fruits start to become overripe, I'll make a compote or jam to use up my fruit. Fruit on the verge of spoiling also works well in a baked quick bread. For fresh veggies I need to use up, I include them in soup. (Ann Adams)

I cook ground meat to use in different meals. Tacos for one meal, then can make Mexican cornbread, taco soup, etc. Easy to prep and turn into another meal that everyone loves. Can even make taco mac, taquitos, taco salad. The options are limitless. (Carmen Walker)

I buy a big container of mixed greens (kale, spinach, and spring salad) and chop it into stackable takeout bowls. I add other chopped vegetables, pumpkin seeds, and dried cranberries. They are ready to go. I can add dressing and some grated parmesan and have an instant lunch for every day of the week. (Michelle Rayburn)

I have a one-week menu that repeats. Same meals. I shop for the two weeks. Chop and freeze half of the produce. Use the remainder of the chopped produce for fresh meals. I use mostly fresh foods, so it can get tricky to keep all the produce fresh. (Sharen Close Pearson)

Visit the local farmers' market at the end of the day and get great deals on organic produce. They mark it down quite a bit because most of it would go to waste otherwise. Sometimes I find a great deal, such as a crate of tomatoes for the price of a pint. When I get more than I can use fresh, I can make sauce for the freezer. (Lisa-Anne Wooldridge)

When I see a good sale on canned or other non-perishable ingredients that I use often (i.e., for chili, sloppy joes, soup recipes, pasta, etc.), I buy twelve of each—enough for one meal a month for the year. Throughout the year, I then plan meals to include what I already have on hand. (Nancy Graves)

Plant a garden. Freeze or can the excess produce that you don't eat fresh. Container gardens work well if you lack adequate space or have physical limitations. (Gina Anderson Stinson)

We buy fruit on sale and immediately take it out of the container, put on a plate/flat container. Refrigerate berries. Store apples/oranges/clementines in a cooler place. Fruit lasts longer that way. I also freeze fruit, such as berries and ripe bananas, individually on a cookie sheet and then put in a freezer bag or glass container together. Use within six months. (Tracey Nielsen)

Several years back, I switched to lean ground turkey for most meals (which I can get at a good price from big box stores). When I do use ground beef, I get a leaner cut of it now. I discovered that I wasn't saving more than a few pennies when I accounted for the loss in volume that 20 percent fat gives you compared to the volume you end up with from a leaner cut. The math on buying the 80/20 and boiling it only worked out for me if I bought it in bulk at a discount store, and even then, the savings was under a dollar. (Lisa-Anne Wooldridge)

STRENGTH TRAINING

I've heard so many excuses regarding why women don't want to do strength training workouts. Instead of resisting it, why not give resistance training a try? (See what I did there with the pun?)

While everyone can benefit from strength training, talk with your doctor about it before you start, especially if you have any health issues or if you haven't exercised in a while. Another expert you might want to consult is a fitness trainer to ensure you are doing the lifts or exercises correctly.

Just as our souls have the opportunity to grow from resistance, our physical strength improves when we give it concentrated resistance. This causes the muscles to contract and improves strength, tone, and endurance. This training requires external resistance of some kind. (We'll discuss types of strength training below.)

One myth is that weightlifting will make females look masculine. If you use low weights, this won't happen. But I'll let you in on a little secret. I love it when my muscles pop out. It's a sign of being toned and putting in the work to train. When I see a muscular woman, I always have mad respect for her dedication and discipline. And as I write this, I've been on a hiatus from the heavy-lifting strength training I used to do, and I'm missing those muscles—the ideal curvy bulges for my body!

How it works

What I'm getting ready to share here is going to sound messed up, but trust me, it works! Strength training causes microscopic tears to the targeted muscle cells. Our amazing bodies quickly repair the intentional damage, creating stronger muscles. Muscle fibers heal and grow when we're not taxing them, so it's important to have planned recovery time between workouts of the same muscle groups.

It only takes two or three twenty- to thirty-minute strength-training sessions per week to gain the benefits. If you choose to lift weights more often, be sure to alternate targeted muscle groups. With so little time necessary for strength training, you still have time to do other forms of exercise (such as cardio) for a well-rounded (or maybe I should say well-defined) approach to fitness.

Benefits

1. **Increases lean muscle mass.** We tend to lose muscle as we age, but strength training can prevent that.[11]

2. **Reduces body fat.** Strength training improves the lean-mass-to-fat ratio.[12]

3. **Prevents injury.** Since muscles support our other soft tissues as well as the scaffolding of our bones, the stronger we are, the more resilient we will be. We are less prone to injury because strong muscles improve our stability.[13] (I don't know about you, but I need this because injuries find me!)

4. **Burns more calories.** The more lean muscle we have, the more calories we burn, even at rest.[14]

5. **Builds stronger bones.** One of the ways we can reduce the risk of osteoporosis is to participate in a strength training program. This improves bone density and reduces the risk of fractures.[15]

6. **Creates better joint flexibility.** Strength training keeps our joints nimble (or at least more so than if we didn't challenge them).[16]

7. **Improves balance.** Strengthening exercises help us keep our balance better through improved proprioception and stability. (Proprioception is the perception or awareness of the position and movement of the body.)[17]

8. **Boosts confidence.** One reason it improves confidence is that we can measure progress quicker here than with some other physical wellbeing choices. It feels good to set challenging goals and achieve positive outcomes.

9. **Tends to soul care.** How is this possible? Strength training is a great way to de-stress. It is my time to retreat from my responsibilities. The activity produces some pretty awesome feel-good endorphins, and it also lessens mental fatigue.

Types of strength training

- **Free weights.** These are weights that aren't attached to apparatus. Includes dumbbells, barbells, and other forms of weight.
- **Weight machines.** This is the equipment where the weight is built into an apparatus designed to target specific muscle groups. It uses adjustable bricks of weight or bands calibrated to create a certain poundage of resistance.
- **Circuit training.** In circuit training, you design a workout that blends endurance training, resistance training, aerobics, and other exercises. A circuit is one set of the routine before starting round two. Usually, there is less time for rest/recovery between exercises and sets so that the heart rate stays elevated. This provides a good blend of cardio and strength training.
- **Pilates.** Pilates involves a system of exercise using specially designed apparatus. It's known to improve strength, flexibility, posture, and mental awareness.
- **Bodyweight fitness workout.** This strength-training exercise program uses the individual's own weight to provide resistance against gravity. Bodyweight exercises improve strength, endurance, speed, flexibility, coordination, and balance.
- **Tabata.** Tabata training is a high-intensity interval training (HIIT) workout featuring exercises that last four minutes. This incorporates bodyweight training plus cardio. It usually requires little or no equipment and can be done anywhere. There are modified exercises to help you still get in a good workout while you are reconditioning. Then you can graduate to more difficult moves.
- **Resistance bands.** A resistance band is an elastic (or rubber) band, strap, or tube used for strength training. Stretching these with our body parts causes muscles to contract and relax. We might be more familiar with using them for physical therapy, but the same principles apply to improving strength. Proper technique is important to avoid injuries. The benefit is you can take the bands wherever you want to work out, and it does not require other equipment.
- **Kettlebells.** Kettlebells are cast iron or cast steel balls with handles attached to the top. Benefits include improved grip strength, better cardio than free-weight lifting, and fewer injuries due to the swinging action of kettlebells providing a more fluid motion.

Terminology

- **Duration.** How long a workout lasts. The time from the beginning of the workout to the end.
- **Rep.** Abbreviation for repetition. The number of times you lift and lower a weight. (Often in one motion or sometimes with a pause at the end of the lift before you bring it back to the start position.) The number of repetitions before you take a break.
- **Set.** A group of reps. If a workout calls for 3 sets of 10 reps (3×10), you'll perform 10 reps of the lift. That's one set. Rest. Perform the second set of 10 reps. Rest. Perform the third set of 10.
- **Failure.** The point in an exercise when your muscles are so fatigued that you can't perform any more reps with proper form. Sometimes workouts tell you to "perform a set until failure." This means you crank out as many full-range-of-motion reps as you can. When you can't do any more in a row, that ends the set. Usually, you wait until the last set in a workout to go to failure. When your muscle quivers, it is warning that you are near failure.

A basic workout

Do eight to twelve repetitions of a strength-training exercise targeting each major muscle group. Incorporate rest between sets for muscle recovery. Use two to four sets per muscle group. Good form is extremely important to prevent injuries. If you are uncertain, arrange for a coaching session. Or video yourself doing the lifts and compare with other videos of those same lifts to make sure you're using proper technique.

Getting started

You can join a gym or set up a workout space in the privacy of your own home (or garage). Research what equipment you need and what lifts/exercises you want to incorporate into your workout. Make a plan that targets each major muscle group. Ideally, some of your exercises will involve more than one body part (called compound lifts) to challenge your anatomy and get to positive outcomes even faster. Look for cross-body motions as well.

What about it? Will you add strength training to your workout program?

PERSONAL STEWARDSHIP CARE PLAN

(This resource goes well with the chapter "Curb Your Attitudes and Actions.")

Self-caregiving

We require the same kind of care a gardener would give a garden to help it have a good outcome. Ignoring our needs ends up as neglect. It takes much longer to get out of a state of being chronically depleted than if we maintain a healthy body, soul, and spirit. Let's faithfully partner with God to take care of our whole being, for his glory. It isn't something we can procrastinate without negative effects.

My personal plan

I spent some time reflecting on how I'm self-caregiving. Out of that time of prayer and pondering came my own personal stewardship care plan. Your plan will look different because you are different. By allowing you to see my plan, it might help you brainstorm your own.

Definitions

Nourish. Feeds what is needed to prevent depletion and to create health and wholeness.

Nurture. Nurses and takes care of what is wounded or weak.

Rest. Pauses to provide a respite for relaxation or sleep.

Refresh. Invigorates by providing opportunities to rejuvenate, energize, and recharge.

Replenish. Replaces what is empty or diminished by filling up, restocking, and topping off.

Before I could come up with my specific caregiving plan, I had to evaluate my intentions based on needs for a healthy body, soul, and spirit.

Body

- I will nourish my body with healthy foods that do not exacerbate my disease processes.
- I will nurture my body by taking care of dental and medical issues.
- I will rest my body by being intentional with sleep hygiene.
- I will refresh my body by pampering it with what makes it feel rejuvenated.
- I will replenish my body by eating more produce (eat the rainbow!).

Soul

- I will nourish my soul by adding intentional joy-makers.
- I will nurture my soul by addressing unhealthy relationship issues.
- I will rest my soul by adding margin into my day.
- I will refresh my soul by fellowshipping with others on a weekly basis.
- I will replenish my soul by experiencing God's beauty weekly.

Spirit

- I will nourish my spirit by meditating on God's Word daily.
- I will nurture my spirit by praying to God regarding all that is on my heart and mind.
- I will rest my spirit by taking timeouts for talking with God multiple times a day.
- I will refresh my spirit by taking time to see God's virtues and worshiping him.
- I will replenish my spirit by growing in grace and in the knowledge of my Lord.

Breaking down specifics

Many of the specific items on my care plan are not fun but are necessary. These are the bare minimums of my maintenance plan so that I don't become depleted in body, soul, or spirit.

Your list will be different. And many of you would be overwhelmed to have twelve details on your maintenance plan at once. It's often more manageable to make a list and then focus on just one item at a time until it becomes a habit. Then move on to a new goal. Give yourself permission to make a list that works for you rather than duplicating (but never implementing) a list similar to mine.

My delightful dozen

1. Take care of dental problems when they arise and maintain dental care with appointments to the dentist and hygienist twice a year.
2. Keep A1C in mind when making food choices. Have it tested three times a year.
3. Have a date with exercise or fitness at least thirty minutes a day, five days a week.
4. Address physical problems with physical therapy at clinic, gym, or home regularly.
5. Take vitamins and supplements daily. *That's why they are called* ***daily*** *vitamins, Kathy!*
6. Do what it takes to get a minimum of seven hours of sleep a night and at least one hour of deep sleep.
7. Make weekly meal plans (recipes, menus, grocery list).
8. Prep ingredients for meals. Make meal-prep "dates" to do ahead of time and incorporate quick meals that require little time.
9. Track food and exercise at least five times a week.
10. Provide intentional activities and breaks for rest and relaxation.
11. Have consistent time with God that provides for wellbeing of spirit and soul. Journal this. (Will involve worship, confession, prayer, study, and meditation.)
12. Read at least two books a month.

I will re-evaluate my list quarterly to update it. Once an intention becomes a lifestyle, I can remove it from focus and add a new intention that needs attention.

For reflection

- Think back to what made wellbeing practices work when I was 100 percent on program. What choices from that time can I add back in to my wellbeing intentions?

- What causes me to go off program? How can I deal with it to get back on track?

- Remember my why!

My Care Plan

BALANCING PRIORITIES

One of the positive traits in successful people is knowing when it's necessary to pivot in a timely and effective manner to stay pointed toward their long-term missions. This is different than the short-term goals. Our to-do lists and short-term goals will change when necessary to get us closer to our lifetime purpose.

It helps me when I have crazy weeks (most weeks lately) to remind myself that my wellbeing (body, soul, and spirit) is the only thing that is going to help the other stuff go better. It's my personal responsibility as an act of stewardship. Letting it slip means the problems are taking over. It's so hard to make this a priority when it feels as if there's nothing left in the tank. But that's when I have to remind myself not to give wellbeing the leftovers but the firstfruits.

Finding balance is about:

- Time discipline
- Work efficiency
- Lowering expectations on what doesn't matter
- Determining when it's okay to multi-task and when you need to mono-task

Procrastination regarding anything in life can cause us to feel stuck or paralyzed with our goals, to-do lists, and wellbeing.

Try this

1. Make a list of anything to do with wellbeing of body, soul, or spirit that you have been delaying or procrastinating.
2. Identify every area you have lost the steam or passion to work on.
3. For each item on the list, decide if the lack of desire to address it is because you got ahead of God in planning it. Maybe you didn't seek his direction first. Or maybe you have too many ideas for wellbeing that need implementing. You can't do them all at once, and you can't decide which one(s) to tackle first. Ask God for his leading.

4. Talk to God now and ask him how he wants you to get out of the mess you made! Then follow the Super D Plan below for each item on the list.

Note: Sometimes, we *did* sense God leading us to set a goal toward wellbeing, but then circumstances outside of our control have changed and we have to let some things go. That's okay! I don't want you to assume each project got bumped due to disobedience to God—sometimes we inherit messes we didn't create.

Super D Plan

DECIDE it:

1. **D**O it. If God leads your heart to believe he wants you to do it, make it a priority. Keep in mind, making choices for good health of body, soul, and spirit are always God's will, but individual ideas toward those goals might change or not be relevant to you.
2. **D**ELAY it. Sometimes it's a great idea, but it's just not time yet. This is different than the lazy procrastination of overwhelm. Example: I joined a gym, and before I got to set up a workout program there, I found out I had some medical issues requiring rest from most exercise while awaiting a surgical consult. It's okay to delay when it isn't the right time.
3. **D**ELETE it. Just don't do it! Isn't it a relief to decide some things just plain ol' don't need to be done? Example: going on that diet sounded good when you signed up for the membership, but it isn't working for you. There are other ways to eat for health. It's okay to cancel the membership if it isn't a good fit.

Your time management system

Will a time management system help you with your sense of overwhelm? Here are a few different ways to tackle your to-do list:

- Do many fast tasks on your list first so you can see progress right away to encourage you for the rest of the day.
- Do the item you tend to procrastinate first. Get it out of the way.
- Do the item that is most pressing first—it has a deadline.

- Do the big item that you neglect because you're busy helping others but is most needful for your own wellbeing. One way to do this is to break it into smaller projects that fit easier into your schedule.
- Designate big chunks of time a few times a month for larger projects that need your full attention. When you do this, you intentionally put blinders on so you aren't distracted by all else. Have a singular focus on the dedicated project.
- Schedule the day based on your energy and mental acuity. Do no-brainer items when you aren't as sharp and the items that need your full focus during the time of day when you can best do them.

Making lists

- Type up a master list of all your projects so you don't forget them, but don't work from this list. The purpose for this list is to prevent worrying about something you need to do later. When your mind tries to distract you because you are afraid that you'll forget to do it, you can remind yourself it's on the list and won't be forgotten. Use the master list to create other lists below.
- Make a quarter-year plan. Divide that into three monthly plans. Use that to create weekly plans. Then come up with the day plan.
- Have a focus of three have-to-do items that you will stay up late or cancel something else in order to get done, then have three other items that might get done if you can, and three items that are floaters for when you get to them. A list of nine things is doable, especially when you give yourself permission to only do three of them.
- When making your list, you'll notice several items occur every day. Unless you have a hard time getting to them, combine them into one entry on your list. Call these your morning habits. They include devotions, getting yourself presentable, straightening the house, looking at your day plan, defrosting food for dinner, social media time, email time, etc.

Guilt and others

- Sometimes we don't make time for our wellbeing because we haven't explained to others that this is a priority to us.
- We feel guilty for taking time to do it when others need us.

- It's time to release the guilt. Time to let go of needing to be needed. And time to tell others what we are working on so they can celebrate the progress we make.
- Keep the vision for our wellbeing in front of those with whom we spend the most time. It helps us stay accountable without feeling guilty for having to decline other uses of our time and energy.

How to keep the vision in front of others

- Announce your wellbeing intention on social media (if you feel comfortable with that).
- In the morning, tell others in your household or workplace what your day holds. If you have anyone who calls or texts daily, tell them so they know you are serious about being focused. Not getting needlessly interrupted helps you complete those goals.
- At mealtime, share the progress you've made, what you've learned in the process, or a struggle you are having with your wellbeing goals. Good communication helps them to know this takes a lot of work as you make it a priority in your life. They may not always be supportive, but at least you aren't expecting them to read your mind regarding your motivation and intentions.
- Ask your prayer team or partners to pray. Give them specifics.
- One caveat: only share this information with those who will respect your intentions. If they tend to derail you, they might not be good to have on your support team.

TO SLEEP, DIVINE!

In previous sections, we discussed the importance of sleep. Yet so many of us struggle to get the right amount of total sleep or enough restorative sleep. It's good to evaluate what you can do to improve your sleep hygiene.

Ideas

- Set a bedtime alarm. This reminds you to go to bed.
- Shut down screen time for the last hour before bedtime.
- Reduce stimulation and lower lighting.
- Restrict caffeine (how much per day and what time of day).
- Limit exercising later in the day.
- De-stress before bedtime with self-care/soul-care.
- Create a sleep environment. This might include relaxing music or white noise. (I run a fan.)
- Take pain relievers at least thirty minutes prior to bedtime, if needed.
- Use a cold pack or heating pad if you need to address painful spots to rest.
- Learn progressive muscle relaxation exercises.
- Set time of last snack. This helps prevent reflux and blood glucose surge.
- Focus on Bible meditation.
- Write in your journal.
- Use an essential oils diffuser. Lavender is one of the beneficial oils for sleep.
- Quit stimulating activity an hour before sleep time.
- Create a cool, dark bedroom.
- Choose a good mattress and pillow.

- Wear the best garment for sleep—or go nude (especially if menopausal).
- Learn the best (for you) sleep positions.

Nighttime wake-ups

Do you wake up during the night and can't get back to sleep? Evaluate if it is caused by:

- Something physical such as pain, a hot flash, or having to use the restroom.
- Something mental/emotional such as having your mind race with thoughts.
- Something spiritual such as feeling guilt or fear.

How to address sleep issues:

- Do an exercise that helps for the kind of sleep problem you have. (Example: gentle stretching.)
- Research natural options such as melatonin or chamomile or other sleep-enhancing teas.
- Wear wrist braces to bed if you have wrist or hand issues.
- Use a sleep app like Fitbit or Apple watch to evaluate your sleep.
- Experiment with body pillows to find the best position to prevent pain and encourage longer times asleep before waking to shift positions.

One of the best ways to take care of yourself is to take care of your rest.

Sleep is as important as any aspect of wellbeing. What will you do to improve your slumber?

SELF-SABOTAGE

Do you stand in the way of your own success? If your behavior interferes with the goals God has given you, you might be dealing with self-sabotage. What do you allow to get in the way of achieving those God-goals?

These behaviors result in self-defeating consequences. It's possible to overcome most forms of self-sabotage, so don't give up! If you find your problems are more than you can address by yourself, it could be time to get help. Consult a professional counselor, set up an appointment with your pastor, or confide in an accountability partner.

Types of self-sabotage

- Procrastination
- Self-medication with drugs, alcohol, stress eating
- Perfectionism
- Doubt
- Imposter syndrome
- Participating in time-robbers
- Interpersonal conflict at work, in the community, online, or at home
- Waiting for "better" timing or opportunity
- Making excuses
- Justifying poor choices or neglect of intended action

- Unawareness of God at work
- Getting ahead of God or not following him
- Saying yes to other things
- Rehearsing regrets
- Over-analyzing
- Clutter/disorganization (can't find what we need)
- Lack of accountability
- Lack of dividing big goals into doable to-dos

Dangers

- You may think the poor choice is too small to have negative consequences or that it might even help you to act on your goals better. (We say a little bit will help us de-stress, and instead, not making it to our goals causes extra stress and piled-on guilt as well. A vicious cycle leading to unnecessary delay or failure.)
- You may do the bare minimum so you stay under the radar. Just floating. Existing, but not thriving. No rewarding outcomes. Just getting by.

There's a concept called "the upper limit" that says our self-sabotage is like a self-imposed glass ceiling, limiting our ability to find happiness or success.

Self-sabotage has been described as trying to saw off the tree limb upon which you're perched.

The why

(You might identify yourself in one or more of these reasons.)

- **Unworthy**. You don't believe you deserve success or happiness. You feel inadequate.
- **Control**. It's easier to control the failure you plan for than to try/risk and explore the unknowns related to the goal. You fear the potential—because it's uncertain—rather than feeling excited. Not working toward your goal is something you can control, so it feels safe.
- **Imposter syndrome.** You feel like a fraud and are afraid others will find out you're not who you say you are. You don't want to be accused of being a fake. You don't believe in yourself (which is really a lack of faith in the gifts and goals God has given you).

- **Self-assigned blame.** It's easier to choose something you can blame for not achieving your goal than to try toward your goal and fail. Self-sabotage provides a scapegoat if things go wrong. (Example: being busy is the scapegoat for not doing the goal, rather than figuring out a way to find time to work on a micro-task of the goal and getting closer to achievement.)
- **Consistency**. You would rather do the same thing over and over again, even if it keeps you from your goals. You enjoy the comfort and safety of familiarity.
- **Victim**. If you've been overlooked, mistreated, or put in a position of a victim before, you might tend to put yourself in that position rather than to allow someone else to ever wound you again. You stay there rather than finding your way out and breaking the cycle.
- **Fear of failure.** You're afraid to attempt the goal and fall short. You don't want to let down yourself and others. It's easier not to try or to create a trap than to get into unfamiliar territory.
- **Fear of success.** If you make your goal, then that creates a new unfamiliar life and new work to maintain. Essentially, you're not sure you have it in you to keep the train in motion once you get it going.
- **Overwhelmed**. You're too stressed or lack the confidence to learn what you need to know to accomplish the intended goal. So rather than deal with the problems holding you back, you create other problems.

Remedies

- Look for your predictable patterns. What is your go-to self-sabotage method? What stinking thinking derails you when you get close to the right path of pursuing your goals?
- What triggers self-sabotage for you? Some examples: lack of rest, lack of clarity, relationship struggle, lack of support, self-doubt, lack of faith.

- Deal with your fears. Evaluate what you are truly afraid of. Face your fears by imagining the worst-case scenario for what might happen, and then determine how you will handle it if the worst does come to pass. Once you see it for what it is, you have victory and can be released from the fear. Trust that Jesus will be your rescuer and protector—or he will simply be with you even in the failure so you are not alone. No matter what, the result is up to God—your part is simply to be obedient and faithful in stepping out as he leads. Don't forget, Jesus also wants to be there for your victories—not just to pick you up when you are down. Strive for those victories! (Can you imagine doing a happy dance with Jesus? Exhilarating!)
- Identify distorted thought patterns. If you aren't familiar with this concept, search the term online for descriptions. Examples: absolutes, personalized blame for all wrongs in life, catastrophizing, overgeneralization, labeling, unrealistic expectations, proving our rightness, jumping to conclusions, fortune-telling, emotional reasoning/not fact-based, shoulds and shouldn'ts, filtering out positive information and magnifying the negative, feeling you deserve rewards that don't come, etc.
- Correct the choices and attitudes that distract and derail you from your goals, leading to doubt and defeated attitudes and actions.
- Confess the problem. One way to honor the struggle but get past it is to bring it into the light and out of the darkness. You can do that with an accountability partner, a mentor or coach, or your pastor.
- Reduce your to-do list. We spend more time and energy on things that do not matter and then stress out when we don't have time or energy for what is most important. We will all face times of overwhelm in our lives, but let's work to diminish how often it stresses us out.
- When you pillow your head at night, celebrate what has been done rather than blaming yourself for what didn't get done or worrying about what is yet to be done. Rest is important for future progress. The only way to achieve that (whether with sleep, peace, or contentment) is to simply rest in Jesus. And the best way to rest in Jesus is after you've spent the day with him!
- Learn to lean on specific spoken intentions and affirmations (as long as they align with God's Word and Spirit).
- Regain motivation using resources that work with your personality type.
- Use tools and computer resources to prevent becoming distracted from your goals.

- Find Bible verses that help you move past the problem and into the solution.
- Seek songs (with a focus on lyrics) that help you release struggles and get closer to victory.
- Set a despite-the-fear type goal to escape the trap and help you step in faith toward your goal.
- Keep your goals ever before you, so you don't mindlessly go through your days wondering why you aren't getting closer to God's purpose for your life.
- Make sure the goals are from God. If they are manmade, with a view of obligation, ought-to-dos, should, expectations, or desire for the world's view of success, they need to go!
- Practice healthy self-care and soul-care.

With the right strategy, we can escape our patterns of self-sabotage and explore new territory beyond that self-imposed upper limit. It's time to stop what's stopping you!

Bible focus:

- *Throw off your old sinful nature and your former way of life, which is corrupted by lust and deception. Instead, let the Spirit renew your thoughts and attitudes* (Ephesians 4:22–23).
- *For God has not given us a spirit of fear, but of power and of love and of a sound mind* (2 Timothy 1:7 NKJV).

Even when you can't tell yourself, "I've got this!" you can tell yourself, "God's got this, and God's got me!"

SNACK TIME

Which snacks require very little prep and won't break the bank? Let's dream up a go-to list.

First, ask yourself these questions

- When I want to snack, what is the reason?
- Is it because what I really need is a breather? (If so, take a break rather than food intake!)
- Do I feel as if I need extra energy? (Food does supply energy but also can cause crashes. What else can give you energy?)
- Am I in a stress-eating spiral out of control? (Deal with the stress, and the hunger might diminish.)
- Is this true hunger or more of an automatic response to typical snack times?

Consider what you're hungry for

Creamy	Sweet
Crunchy	Refreshing
Chocolatey	Sour
Salty	Protein-rich

If you really want one of these types of food but try to avoid it, you might end up eating something that doesn't satisfy you and then go back to eat something that isn't as healthy to appease a craving. By having a variety of healthy snacks, you will feel content without eating more than you've planned.

(As an aside, I've learned that it's okay to be hungry sometimes. I don't neglect what my body needs, but I can be hungry and wait for a planned snack or meal. This is a temporary denial of self in exchange for a long-term positive change for health. I also confess—I'm not completely victorious in this matter!)

Snack Ideas:

Be aware of serving sizes and portions.

- Cheese crisps
- No-bake energy balls
- Muffins packed with healthy ingredients (like Hulk muffins)
- Trail mix to fit your plan
- Cheese and crackers
- Mandarin orange or clementine
- Banana with peanut butter
- Beef (or other types of) jerky
- Edamame
- Sausage balls made with almond flour
- Apple with nut (or seed) butter or cheese
- Popcorn
- Veggies with healthy dip, hummus, or nut butter
- Nuts (a mixture or all one kind—keep to just one-fourth cup)
- Olives or pickles
- Charcuterie
- Plain yogurt with fresh fruit and a drizzle of honey or maple syrup
- Pepperoni crisped in the microwave
- Smoothie
- Avocados or guacamole with veggies

Check my website at kathycarltonwillis.com to get a free download for some of these recipes. Add your favorites to the list and brainstorm some new ones to try.

SELF-CARE / SOUL-CARE

Self-care isn't selfish. It's a necessary personal stewardship care plan so you can be at your optimal best to serve God and serve others while enjoying a rewarding, refreshing, abundant life. It must be scheduled, or it won't happen!

1. Designate a quiet space away from others. Everyone needs this.
2. Eat a wholesome breakfast to start the day off with extra energy—it also gives you some mental space to start the day with a healthy focus.
3. Create a warm and cozy break. You could pick from these: light a fire, drink a warm beverage, inhale a welcoming scent, cuddle with a blanket, wear a fuzzy/fleecy wrap or slipper socks, read a lighthearted book, etc.
4. Burn a pleasing candle. The scent is nice, yes. But there's something about the flickering flame that is calming. (Even better, get the Woodwick flickering fireside candle for a special sound effect.)
5. Focus on biblical meditation: Bible verses, reflection, God-focused music, and prayer time.
6. Explore something you've never visited in your own town or nearby. (Tourist for a day.)
7. Read back through old letters and notes. I keep a file of compliments others send my way and heartwarming letters. One is a paper file, and one is a digital file. A friend told me these are sometimes called "Smile Files," which as The Grin Gal, I appreciate!
8. Look through old photos. Allow "all the feels."
9. Lie flat on your back and look up in the sky. During the day, watch the clouds and imagine what the shapes could be. During the nighttime, stargaze.
10. Be mindful of something you normally do mindlessly. Be all in. (Example: I'm going to make bread from scratch and savor all the senses.)
11. Watch a series from beginning to end, but not all at once!
12. Play. Be silly. Laugh. Repeat.

13. Give yourself a facial or other indulgent care.
14. Breathing exercises (deep cleansing breaths, not Lamaze).
15. Listen to a different style of music and allow yourself to be immersed in the experience or put on background music and focus on something completely different.
16. Take the stairs or the farthest parking lot and be mindful during your time getting from point A to point B.
17. Add your favorite fruit to your drinking water.
18. Fill in the blank: "If I were selfish, I would . . ." Then, if it's within your power and means (and doesn't violate your Christian values), do it.
19. Turn off the volume on your devices so you avoid notifications during a mental break. Email, social media notifications, and texts can wait for you.
20. Declutter in short bursts of time. Sometimes clutter creates a sense of overwhelm, and dealing with it gives a sense of order—making everything right with the world. (Not really, but a feeling of that!)
21. Eat something different. We need more variety when our life feels same. Same. Same.
22. Listen to music. Sing or dance to it if you dare.
23. Remove negative people from your social media feed (You can unfollow and not unfriend them, if you prefer, or snooze them for thirty days).
24. Handwrite a note and put it in the outgoing mail.
25. Take an online tour of a museum or amusement park (or go in person if that is suitable for you).
26. Learn a new hobby or skill through an online course or YouTube.
27. Read for entertainment.
28. Spend some time in nature.
29. Enjoy gardening or indoor plants (like a faery garden).
30. Write down your stresses, fears, or other emotions. Then burn the paper and sprinkle the ashes somewhere symbolic.
31. Write an accountability partner with your struggles and victories. Also include aha! moments.
32. Journal.

33. Pet a dog or other cuddly animal.
34. Get a mani-pedi or facial. (You can go to a beauty school for a budget day at the spa.)
35. Say no.
36. Take an exercise or dance class.
37. Walk around your yard or your neighborhood. Be on the lookout for beauty. Say what you spot out loud (like a slug bug game). Thank God for what you see.
38. Color.
39. Remove something from your to-do list that you've procrastinated "forever" by giving yourself permission not to do it. Let it go, delegate it, or hire it done to create more margin in your life.
40. Soak in some sun rays for fifteen minutes (use sunscreen if necessary).
41. Nap (or at least get horizontal).
42. Laugh. Watch a video, a show, or read some silly memes.
43. Use an essential oil diffuser.
44. Take another route to work. Change up your routine.
45. Limit time on social media newsfeeds where negativity hangs out. Instead, go to the pages of people you want to check on or who are uplifting. Give a virtual hug or receive one by writing or reading something that cares for your soul.
46. Soak in a relaxing bath.
47. Slather on an exquisite body product all over. Lavish in the luxury of it.
48. Learn some stretches that target the parts of your body that hold on to stress and take breaks to do these stretches. Or practice progressive muscle relaxation.
49. Take your camera for an outing. Explore cityscapes, architecture, industrial lines, faces, or nature.
50. Make plans for a special day off or weekend. (Mundane days off, doing mundane tasks, can sometimes lead to feeling blah. Do your day-off chores during your regular workweek to give yourself extra space for something special on your day off.)

THE PROBLEM WITH PLATEAUS IS . . .

I asked my Facebook friends to fill in the blank from this headline. See if you relate to any of these.

- Something is happening that I can't see—a new success or failure may be just around the corner. They require patience and perseverance. (Stephenie Hovland)
- They are so hard to get off of. (Jennifer Salyer)
- You lose sight of the finish line. (Janice Hannah Thompson)
- They seem to stretch on forever. (Jessica Caudill)
- There is no growth. (Crystal Smith-Coleman)
- The amount of work required to keep motivation alive. There's no motivation quite like success. (Leisa Riley Stokes)
- They quickly bring discouragement if we are not on guard against them. (Edwina Cowgill)
- They occur due to complacency or becoming comfortable with our accomplishments, and we gradually lose our desire to put forth the effort it takes to succeed. They sneak up on us. (Ann Adams)
- The realization that the only energy left for us to expend—still in our control—is in waiting, or standing still, or having patience; an often spiritually and/or emotionally uphill battle in itself. (Nancy Graves)
- You start feeling comfortable in that place and stop pushing as hard for the finish. (Tami Lockard)
- So frustrating because you fall into bad habits! You need a kick in pants to motivate to a higher goal! (Amy Goettsch Franckowiak)
- They require patience and diligence without an immediate reward. We like microwavable progress! (Edna Earney)

- There is a danger of falling into complacency. Complacency can easily turn us away from our goals and growth, and we begin to lose our footing. How long before a plateau becomes a cliff? (Alicia Willsie)
- I fear the plateau is a sign of imminent failure. (Judy Isaacs Herrig)
- That we tend to linger too long in that level place. A plateau is meant for rest and renewal. It's not meant to be a place where we linger, grow complacent, stop exercising our faith muscle, or stop moving forward in our faith walk. (JoAnn Reno Wray)
- They may stop your momentum. (Janet Pierce)
- They tempt you to rest too long; another climb is always on its way. (Sharon Elliott)
- They stop you flat without any ups or downs, so they bore you. (Janyce Brawn)
- The view isn't usually great. (Donna Safford)
- You have to outsmart yourself in a new way each time. (Tracey Nielsen)
- People are tempted to give up and lose hope. (Lucy Ann Moll)
- They're so comfy. (Dee Smith)

MARGIN

The best way to add margin to our lives is to let go of finding identity and purpose in being busy. What does accomplishing more get you? If out of balance, it can get you more health problems, more stress, and more commitments. (I'm not saying to be lazy—but there is a balance.)

Busyness might be a status symbol of success with today's culture, but that is not how God designed us.

God doesn't *value* us more when we *do* more. Papa God treasures our time with him and our work in loving others well.

When we face our emotional, physical, and spiritual health head-on, we see the need for margin. What is margin? It's adding space in our day to breathe. Even though it seems as if having that space should be a freedom, it actually requires boundaries. If we don't intentionally make room to reverse the damage of overdoing it, we will keep on overdoing it! Margin is the space between healthy demands in a day and maxed-out resources. You might be able to overdo it for the short-term to get through a crunch period, but it's never wise to allow that pace to continue.

The long-term risk of being too busy is burnout. One way to avoid this is to build rest into our schedule. This involves setting boundaries and not taking on too many commitments. It also requires discipline to spend less time on some tasks, realizing they can easily overtake our days with unnecessary wheel-spinning (like the hamsters, going round and round but not getting anywhere).

If you feel like you are suffocating in overwhelm and weighed down in pressures, you are a prime candidate for needing more margin. Something has to go, or you will be depleted with low reserve. It reminds me of the time my blood work showed I had the proper amount of iron, but when the doctor did a bone marrow biopsy, he found I had zero iron in reserve. They said this meant I had enough in circulation for the moment, but if anything at all required more of me, I'd be deathly sick.

Just as we need iron in our "bank," we need to keep some energy and mental focus reserved for emergencies and high-demand situations. It's the same concept as having an emergency financial fund for when an appliance goes out. We can survive without the extra funds, but it leaves us scrambling to figure out a way to make it work. We don't like that in finances *or* in our lives!

What we do with our margin is just as important as making sure we have space in our day for wellbeing. It's time to regroup and let your mind refocus. What helps you get refreshed? Usually, it requires living in the moment—not looking back with regrets, or meeting overdue deadlines, and not looking ahead with worry or plans.

Break the Cycle

How will you get out of the habit of busyness and create a new habit of margin?

Margin-building, busy-breaking tips

Tip 1: Make a to-do list (see "Balancing Priorities" in the resource section). Then remove one item from the list. This begins to set the priority for margin. It's like what Coco Chanel said about editing accessories, "Before you leave the house, look in the mirror and take one thing off."[18] Less is more. Before you start your day, take one thing off your list.

Tip 2: Schedule breaks. This gives you some buffer if you underestimated how long a task would take. But it also enforces the need for breathing room. During a day plan, the break might just be fifteen minutes. During a week plan, you might like to set aside a couple of hours. And once a month, you might need to designate a half-day for margin. If you don't schedule it, it isn't likely to happen. The other tasks will absorb the time—taking however long you have available.

Tip 3: If you have two tasks that take twenty minutes each, go ahead and schedule the two for an hour time slot. This gives you some time to recalibrate, make a phone call, have a potty break, walk in the yard, etc. If you have three tasks that take sixty minutes total and you've not scheduled a buffer zone, you will go into the next hour of work feeling depleted and as if you are behind. This is a recipe for stress. The more stress, the less productive you are. Not to mention, it does a number on your emotions and your mental acuity. (If we complete have-to projects early, we can move on to want-to projects with the extra space in our day.)

Tip 4: Add creativity back into your life. Stressed people often are so busy they've given up all of their hobbies. What is something you would like to do "if you had time"? Make time! Your other obligations will thank you because you show up contented and refreshed rather than overwhelmed and stressed.

Tip 5: Create a morning routine. This starts the night before. Make tomorrow's to-do list before you go to bed. Set out your clothing. Set your alarm and your coffee timer. Plan your meals and snacks. If you do all that, when you wake up, you can engage in your morning routine without any set-up required. What is involved in a morning routine? Each one varies but might include:

- Spending quiet time with God in prayer and Bible reading
- Exercising
- Drinking caffeine
- Getting presentable
- Straightening a section of your house
- Checking email and social media
- Taking vitamins

Tip 6: Schedule a social media time slot. If you don't have a set time for it, you will scroll endlessly, thinking you are unwinding. Instead, you are getting more and more overwhelmed. It will easily fill whatever time allotment you give it. Set a timer if necessary.

Tip 7: Allot a bounce-back day after a period of taxing activity (mentally or physically). We make the mistake of trying to tackle the next thing on the schedule without refueling. I designate these recovery days on my calendar after I travel, after a speaking program, after hosting guests, and after a busy work season. If I do this, I can enjoy the day the way I want. If I don't do this, I tend to find myself sick or injured because I've pushed myself too far. I still have to take time off to recover, but I don't get to enjoy it if I'm sick!

Do you feel as if everyone wants a piece of you, but no one is satisfied with the amount of "you" you designate for their needs? There's a reason for the term *100 percent.* There's nothing more you can get from someone than that. If you try to add in extras to your day, you can't exist at 120 percent. Something has to give. And usually, it's us. Broken down and worn out, we finally get that break we've been longing for. Only now, we're in bed from an injury, illness, or mental breakdown. Let's not push ourselves to the limits or let others do that to us.

By adding margin to our days, we can add meaning to our lives.

Adding buffer zones starts with a choice to say no to other demands and say yes to living in the moment.

PREPARING FOR THE HOLIDAYS

I love the holidays. And unfortunately, I inherited the food-as-a-love-language gene from both sides of my family. I'm finding a variety of methods to enjoy the holidays without setting back my health and weight-loss progress. Sometimes, implementing what I know goes better than at other times! Accountability helps. And keeping close touch of my *why.*

Perhaps focus group member Kristine Accola said it best when she reminded us, "It's called holi*day*, not holi*weeks*." Savor the flavors for your holiday meal but not for weeks on end of "the holidays." Just because Thanksgiving and Christmas are close together on the calendar doesn't mean we should give up our goals for that entire time. Let's be mindful to eat well when we're celebrating but eat for *being* well the other meals.

One thing I hate, but that helps, is scheduling bloodwork and doctor visits between Thanksgiving and the end of the year. I want my test results to be as good as possible—and that number on the scale, too.

While others are gaining the holiday five to ten pounds, my goal is to hold my own. In Kathy-math, that's like losing during other times of the year. That way, when I dive into "getting back on track" on January 2, I don't have that extra holiday weight to lose as others do. See? It's a win! I'll be ahead of the game. What is your holiday strategy?

One of my holiday meal plans is to allow myself to eat the holiday dishes that we don't commonly have on our table throughout the year. My family thinks you need sweet potatoes *and* mashed white potatoes for Thanksgiving. They want the mashed as a food vessel for their gravy. I've decided I can forego the mashed potatoes on my plate even if they're on the table, knowing I can have them next time we have roast or meatloaf. I also know that homemade yeast rolls are only made a few times a year, so it's worth not eating other carbs to enjoy those fluffy orbs of goodness. To offset that, I choose the pumpkin pie option and don't eat the pie crust. Sometimes, I even make a sugar-free crustless pumpkin pie. I don't miss the crust and sugar! And really, the other ingredients are good for you.

Here are some more tips

- If you're going to a buffet or potluck, look over the whole food line before choosing which ones you'll put on your plate. Better to savor some of the food than be miserable after eating all of the food.
- Eat slowly, enjoying conversation as much as the food. Ask others questions and invest in truly listening. Reminisce favorite family memories. Tell younger generations stories of their ancestors.
- After you finish your plate of food, offer to serve others. Refill glasses. Delay seconds or dessert. Let your food have time to catch up with you so your brain starts to register that you are getting full.
- When you decide you are finished, pop a mint or piece of gum to freshen your breath. Put on some lipstick. You're less likely to want to mess that up with more food!
- Choose extra activity to offset the extra food intake. Make group activities a new family or friend tradition. Go to an area known for Christmas lights. Park the car and walk as a group to see the decorations. Be sure to have on light colors or reflective gear so you don't get hit, and carry a flashlight. Or think ahead and give everyone in the group a glow necklace to wear. (Or even some twinkly Christmas light necklaces!) Go to a pecan orchard and pick up nuts.
- Bring a healthy recipe option to carry-in dinners. Make it so good, others can't believe it's healthy. They'll start asking for it at future gatherings.
- Make the non-food parts of the holiday shine more. Focus on the love. Make new memories.
- Have a plan for the day before and after a holiday to eat more produce and proteins. Clean eating helps offset one day of savoring special foods.
- Make an extra effort to get more sleep. We need it more than ever during the holidays, and it truly is one thing that affects wellbeing of body, soul, and spirit.
- If you are diabetic, check your blood glucose so that number is front and center as you eat. Try to achieve a good average as you evaluate what your blood glucose does at different times of day (fasting, postprandial, random).
- Think about what your favorite food is for each holiday, and make sure you get to enjoy that dish by denying yourself some of the other choices. Again, it's about savoring what goes into your mouth and then being sentimental regarding non-food holiday choices.

At a time of year when we have a lot on our plates, we need to make sure we don't pile a lot on our dinner plates! And for that matter, we need to reduce what we have on our life plates too—so we can truly savor the season.

BACK TO THE GYM

After taking time off due to circumstances outside of my control, I'm going back to the gym for my workouts. As you've read elsewhere in this book, I've enjoyed being a gym rat before, even though I'm not athletic in mindset or build. As much as I anticipated my return and had a heart of gratitude when the time was right to go back, I experienced gym "heartburn" before I even got there. I figure if I had a hard time despite my love of gym life, others reading this might have similar struggles.

Reasons it was hard

- I wanted to grab a bag and go. But when the time was best to get in my first workout, I had nothing prepared ahead of time. I grabbed my iPad to read a book while on the treadmill and discovered there was zero charge. I spent time looking for an unread paper book in my collection and grew impatient. I grabbed my earbuds to listen to music instead. But then I looked at my phone for a good workout playlist and realized none of my music transferred over from my last phone. I didn't have any audiobooks or podcasts loaded either.
- I didn't have a workout planned ahead of time.
- I was going to an unfamiliar gym. The equipment was different. The people were different. Nothing was the same as my prior gym experiences.
- I was taking an older woman to the gym—me! I'm the oldest I've ever been (we all are, at this moment, obviously). I realized quickly it would be unfair to expect myself to pick up where I left off at the gym since so much time has passed. What I'm able to do today can't compete with my personal best, and I shouldn't expect that of myself!
- My Fitbit wristband broke, and I couldn't find the package of new ones I bought. I didn't want to hold my phone the whole time to use the tracker there. I just had to tell myself that exercise counts whether it's counted or not!

I'm writing this after my first day back to the gym. I had mixed results.

First off, the fingerprint reader keypad rejected my scan, so I was locked out until someone coming out let me in. She said she couldn't get it to work either. Then, I tried the scanner to get to the women's-only gym, and that machine wasn't working either. So, I had to go to the co-ed section. At previous gyms, I used the co-ed option because there's a good energy there and better equipment. When I bought my membership at this new location, the gym manager said the women's side is never used. My plan was to go there since I wanted to ease back into working out again and not be around a lot of people. Instead, I had to adjust my mind to going to the co-ed side. I did it!

I found a treadmill, got on it, and figured out the settings (different than the five other types I've used prior). It wasn't user-friendly, so setting the speed was no simple task. Once I got it adjusted, my mph rate was lower than I had hoped it would be, meaning I will need to get better conditioned. It wasn't an awful rate but had gone down a few points from my best, despite breaking a sweat with my outdoor and at-home walking program.

My intention was to explore the rest of the gym, take photos of the equipment, then come home to make a workout plan. After all those mind drains and setbacks, I didn't do that. While I was on the treadmill, I did look through the mirror to the machines behind me to get the lay of the land. I used that time to survey who else was there and their level of fitness. I had to do some positive biblical self-talk regarding comparisons. I'm sure the more I go to the gym, the more confidence I'll pick up. The good news is, I got in thirty minutes on a machine demanding much of me—I'm proud of that! It will take time. (I'm also dealing with a disease flareup, so I need to gradually increase exercise in order to not cause a setback or injury.)

Why do I share my struggle? Because I know if it was hard for me—someone who loves the gym—it might be hard for some of you. I evaluated what could have gone better. Here is what I decided.

Remember getting ready for the first day of school (or getting your children ready)? We didn't wake up one day and just head to school with zero preparation. Moms often bought or sewed our new school clothes, purchased school supplies found on the list the teacher provided, and tried to get everything together we'd need to be ready. (Garage sales were frequented as often as buying new from the stores.) We started going to bed earlier and discussed what to expect once we got to school. The school administrators gave us a tour of the school so we'd know where our classes were. We met our teachers, and we talked about which other students might be in class with us. The night before going back, we set out our clothes and packed our backpacks so we would have less hassle the first morning of school. I realize my recollection of school prep might be different than yours, but it ties in well to getting ready to go back to the gym.

Going back to something we were once familiar with still takes mental and physical preparation. (And if you're going for the first time, even more so!)

Prepping for the gym

Your list will be different than mine, but here are some things to consider when prepping for the gym.

1. What clothing do you need to feel and function your best? Undergarments that support, breathe, and wick moisture. Tops and bottoms that fit your body right now, not the body you hope to be or the body you used to be. Socks that prevent blisters. Shoes that work for you. (Don't wait to buy something new. You can find something on hand that works for comfort. It isn't a fashion show!)
2. Do you need something to occupy your attention while your body works? You don't always need this, but if it helps you spend more time exercising, you might like music, reading material, podcasts, TV shows, etc.
3. If you are shy, invite a friend to go with you. I don't know anyone in my new community yet, so it's possible my next new friend is already going to the gym, and I just need to be confident and say hello.
4. Take a filled water bottle. Drink before you're thirsty.
5. Stash a dry hand towel in your go-bag. You can use it to wipe down machines or to wipe down *you!*
6. Add some lip balm to your gym bag. Lips dry out while you work out.
7. Include whatever you need to freshen up afterward, ranging from showering at the gym and having a full change of clothes to a simple comb to get you home.
8. Pack a little treat to reward yourself after your workout. It could be as simple as a stick of sugar-free gum or a protein bar or shake. (Something on your eating plan, of course!)

Ideas for getting back in the groove at the gym

- Set up a one-time coaching with the fitness instructor to get familiar with the equipment and come up with a plan. (This is hard for me because I used to be able to create workout plans for other people and show them how to use the equipment with proper form.)

- Address my mindset. Pride and insecurity might seem to be at opposite ends of the spectrum, but I'm experiencing both struggles. I need to adjust my mental perspective before I open the door to the gym next.
- Pack a go-bag with all the supplies I need to make working out a good experience.
- Have a gradual approach to getting back in gear. A soft launch. Each time, explore one more machine. Create a sliding-scale-type workout plan that increases the intensity and the variety of exercise a little at a time.

I didn't anticipate my gym return to challenge me as it did. I wasn't prepared for the mental part of going back. Want to know what I learned?

Even when it doesn't go exactly according to plan—do it *messy*! It's still making progress compared to waiting to do it right.

What is your action plan to help you get to your next hard thing? It might be the gym or something else entirely. We need to approach it like we do everything else, with heart, soul, strength, and mind. When we're prepared, we're equipped to overcome obstacles. But don't wait for a perfect day. Be willing to start today and make messy progress.

THE GRIN GAL'S PLANNER FOR WELLBEING

The Grin Gal's Planner for Wellbeing

A 90-Day Habit Tracker for Being Well in Body, Soul & Spirit

This 90-day habit tracker can be used in conjunction with *The Grin Gal's Guide to Wellbeing* book or separately. Customize the pages to fit what you need for your wellbeing journey. It is designed to help you grow in your personal stewardship. You'll find motivational quotes to fuel your wellbeing choices.

Pages offer guidance to include intentions that pursue wellness and wholeness of your body, soul, and spirit. This isn't just about weight loss or physical accomplishments. The inner being needs to be nourished and exercised too. Use the space as a planner or a journal—whatever works best to help propel you toward your goals.

The daily pages have sections for food and fitness. You might want to use these as a planner to figure out your meals and exercises ahead of time. Or, if you prefer, use it as a habit tracker to document after the fact.

If you are creative, decorate the pages with colorful markers, doodles, tape, stickers, etc. If you are more of a bare-bones minimalist, use simple bullets to organize your space. Whatever works for you, put it to work for you!

(Case Laminate Hardcover)

Included in the planner

Daily

- Habit Tracker for Food (Breakfast, Lunch, Dinner, Snacks)
- Habit Trackers for Water and Fitness
- Mood for Day
- Prayer Focus
- Bible Verse Focus
- End of Day Check-Up

Weekly

- End of Week Look Back
- Weight
- Victories
- Aha! Moments
- Next Week Look Forward
- Self-Care / Soul-Care
- Goals & Plans

Monthly

- Measurements
- Non-Scale Victories
- Goals
- I Want to Try (new ideas)

Quarterly

- Unpack
- Plan

Date *January 3*

Prayer Focus

Father, I dedicate today to glorify you in my body, soul, and spirit. Help me not get sidetracked.

Mood for Day

Hopeful

Flexible space for prayer journaling, mindset tracking, and more!

Bible Verse Focus

Hebrews 13:21 — "May he equip you with all you need for doing his will. May he produce in you, through the power of Jesus Christ, every good thing that is pleasing to him. All glory to him forever and ever! Amen."

Fitness

30 minutes HIIT-treadmill

10 minutes moderate, exercise bike

Sleep: 8.3 hours

Water

8 cups! Yay!

FOOD	
BREAKFAST	Protein Bar
LUNCH	Jalapeno popper chicken salad on lettuce, clementine
DINNER	Pork chop, baked sweet potato, butter, green beans
SNACKS	Energy balls, cheese crisps, banana

End of Day Check-Up

- I felt God's presence today.
- Less brain fog.
- More energy.
- I acted on my intentions even though I didn't feel like it.
- I want to not vent to a friend or snack before talking to God about my stressor.
- God's strength equips me when I feel weak.

ACKNOWLEDGMENTS

You know how we have prayer lists with people's names for whom we're praying? Consider this my praise list with names of the people for whom I'm thanking God! I'm sending grateful gratitudes to the following:

Mom. You showed me early on the joy of relishing in fresh food from the garden. Now, whenever I go to a farmers' market, I think of your beautiful gardens and the hard work you put in to make sure we had a well-balanced diet. By canning and freezing the crops, you extended the life of our bounty.

My Wellbeing Warriors focus group. Kristine Accola, Tammy Anderud, Darla Grieco, Stephenie Hovland, Diana Leigh Matthews, Kathy Perrine, Gina Stinson. You stuck with me as I wrote the book and presented it chapter by chapter to you for feedback. You highlighted standout quotes, marked up the sentences that were read-blocks, while also pursuing your own transformation of body, soul, and spirit. Probably what blessed me most was how you supported each other through the vulnerable times of accountability. I hope future groups using the book will gain even more benefits because of the work this first group put in.

My faith family at Praise Church. For 90 percent of the time writing this book, my connection to church was all virtual. The pandemic would have been lonely without the available fellowship, inspiration, and tools for spiritual growth. What I offer others in the way of spiritual guidance is due in part because of what my church poured into me during this time.

My wisdom team. You support me with your notes, calls, prayers, and wise words. Special acknowledgment goes to Jessica Caudill, Sally Ferguson, Stephenie Hovland, Michelle Rayburn, Laurie Ritchel, Robin Steinweg, Gina Stinson, and Lisa-Anne Wooldridge.

Sarah Martinez. You came into my life right when I needed it—when I hit a plateau and also developed new physical issues. Thank you for spending almost two years advising me and providing extra accountability. Your background in anatomy and fitness, coupled with your compassionate ear, provided just what I needed!

WordGirls writing group. You cheered me on as I reported in with each goal and progress report. I wish for you as many writing credits as you pursue!

Joy Weese Moll, my writing buddy. I appreciate the accountability you gave me to keep moving forward despite the obstacles we both faced during the creation of this book project. I don't take it lightly that you've been an almost daily presence in my life for over ten years. Saying I'm grateful just doesn't express it well! Not only did you help me stay focused with the writing, but your own wellbeing journey inspired me as I pursued mine!

My editor and book designer, **Michelle Rayburn**. Thank you for being the creative force behind my Grin Gal brand. Your attention to editing details matched with your design skill deliver a quality product every single time. Also, you get a second thank you because of your accountability, insight, and motivation through this wellbeing process. It doesn't go unnoticed that you took time away from your own goals to help me with mine.

My husband, Russ. You are one of the reasons I want to pursue wellbeing of body, soul, and spirit. You bring quality of life to my days, and I want to give you the most days of my life possible. We started the wellbeing pursuit during a dark time in our lives. One of my favorite memories of that difficult season was working out with you in the gym together. Thank you for propelling me forward.

Jesus Christ, my Savior and Lord. The only reason I'm here is because of you. I pray you are pleased with my pursuit of wellbeing. Thank you for equipping me with all the tools I need for personal stewardship so I can take care of the one "me" I get here on earth. Use this book for your good purposes and glory.

ABOUT THE AUTHOR

God's Grin Gal, Kathy Carlton Willis, writes and speaks with a balance of funny and faith, whimsy and wisdom. She coaches others to remove the training wheels of doubt and not just risk but also take pleasure in the joy ride of life. She is known for her debut book, *Grin with Grace* and for her grinning Boston Terrier, Hettie.

Not many funny girls also have Bible degrees! She graduated with honors from Bible college, holding degrees in Bible and church education, and served for thirty years in full-time church ministry with her pastor/husband, Russ. She's active as a book industry pro while also staying involved in her church.

Kathy works with women's groups and writers' groups, inside and outside of the church. She's passionate about helping believers have *aha! moments* with the daily application of Scripture.

Even with all the circumstances she's faced, she gives a clear message that she possesses an expectant hope and contentment in the Lord. Something we can all experience.

Kathy Carlton Willis owns KCW Communications, spinning many plates as writer, editor, speaker, and coach. Over 1,000 of her writing projects have appeared online and in print publications.

CBN.com features Kathy's popular blog. *CBN* consistently ranks among the top ten most popular sites in the Lifestyle–Religion category. *Grin and Grow with Kathy* offers a twice-monthly devo-study utilizing her story, study, and steps format.

She is a contributing writer for *Upgrade Your Life, The Christian Communicator, The Christian Pulse*, along with others. Kathy also writes inspirational, motivational, and transparent posts and videos on social media.

Kathy founded WordGirls, a community of Christian female writers who receive professional coaching from Kathy.

She identifies issues that hold believers back and her words illuminate their paths to freedom. Kathy reflects God's light during speaking programs as well as one-on-one counseling.

Learn more at Kathy's website: **kathycarltonwillis.com**

OTHER TITLES FROM 3G BOOKS

In addition to ***The Grin Gal's Guide to Wellbeing***, Kathy Carlton Willis has a full line of books. Kathy's boldly practical tips, tools, and takeaways show up in Christian living books, Bible studies, and devo-studies. 3G Books are perfect for small groups or individual reading.

7 Trials Every Woman Faces

Struggling with life challenges? You are not alone!

Ever wish for a friend who really understood you? *7 Trials Every Woman Faces* offers a virtual friend to lean on. Kathy comes alongside you as she shares insights learned through her own stinky situations.

All life trials fit in the same categories as Job's afflictions (told in the oldest book of the Bible). Whenever Kathy feels as if there's a "kick me" sign on her back, she asks, "Is Job a member of my family tree?" Laughing helps a little.

The chapter segments go along with the family tree theme:

- Family Album. Snapshots of heartwarming stories from real life.
- Family Bible. Biblical insights to overcome trials from a godly perspective.
- Family Recipes. Practical steps to help you grow and succeed God's way.
- Family Legacy. Lessons passed along as you help others endure trials.

Learn how to overcome Job-like trials when your family lets you down, friends misunderstand you, your health crumbles, your finances plummet, or others question your faith.

Everyone has trials, but it's the way we deal with hardship that determines not only the outcome but how we cope when we're smack-dab in the middle of them.

Praise for the book:

7 Trials Every Woman Faces is filled with wisdom. Kathy is an experienced guide who brings hope, help, and a ray of sunshine to brighten the rocky road you may be on. This book not only helps readers learn to cope but shows us how to help others suffering.

—Pam Farrel, author of 50+ books including bestselling *Discovering Hope in the Psalms*, co-director of Love-Wise.com

Incredibly practical and unfortunately relevant, *7 Trials Every Woman Faces* offers come-alongside wisdom, laughter, and plenty of application. Who knew Job could be so fun? Seriously, you'll giggle, grimace, and then shift to gratitude that you can work through this current batch of trials with a good friend.

—Jane Rubietta, international speaker and author of zillions of words, including *Brilliance: Finding Light in Dark Places*

This book is that companion you need to walk you through the trials of your present season. Kathy uses honest storytelling, humor, and solid theology to guide all of us on our Job-like journeys to a posture of hope.

— Dorina Lazo Gilmore-Young, author, speaker, contributor for DaySpring's (in)courage, Widow Mama Collective

With Kathy's uplifting stories and insightful Bible teaching, I believe *7 Trials Every Woman Faces* will become the go-to book for thriving in the midst of trials. Kathy walks readers by the hand through their struggles and gives them a new perspective. I especially like the section on difficult conversations. When you face uncomfortable situations head-on, you really can grin again!

—Linda Goldfarb, author of the *LINKED Quick Guide to Personalities* series, board-certified Christian life coach

The Grin Gal's Guide to Joy

If you've ever felt like the joy, joy, joy, joy down in your heart has gone missing, then this book is for you!

Kathy learned that happiness runs and hides, but joy remains when trials show up. Now she's here to share these principles with you in *The Grin Gal's Guide to Joy.*

In each chapter:

- Grin with Joy tells real-life stories and observations. You'll laugh at Kathy's humorous confessions and wacky insights.
- Grow with Joy features a joy word study and workbook. Kathy explores what the Bible says and unpacks timely truths.
- Go with Joy offers life application. Pick the action steps that help you live a joy-filled life.
- Give with Joy equips you to share joy and meet the needs of others. This is when faith becomes ministry.
- Your Grin with Joy Challenge describes a joy-challenging scenario to solve.

Praise for the book:

With her trademark honesty, warmth, wit, and humor, Kathy inspires us to grin with joy, regardless of our circumstances.

—Christin Ditchfield, radio host, speaker, and author of over 80 books

Kathy Carlton Willis writes stories from her open-book life in a way that makes me want to say, "She gets me! She really really gets me!"

—Pat Layton, author, *Life Unstuck*

With relatable stories of finding joy even in the challenges of life, Kathy leads the way with wonderful humor and refreshing honesty. Her joy is infectious!

—Julie Zine Coleman, speaker, author, and managing editor

Kathy is humorously serious about joy! She doesn't just tell us why we can grin with joy; she shows us how to go out and live joyfully.

—Kathy Howard, speaker, Bible teacher, and author

The Ultimate Speaker's Guide

The first book to kick off 3G Books was created with speakers in mind. Packed cover-to-cover with invaluable information, *The Ultimate Speaker's Guide* is the new bible for communicators.

With almost two decades of industry knowledge under her belt, Kathy Carlton Willis has coached hundreds of speakers to help them develop successful speaking businesses. This book covers all the tips, tools, and takeaways you'll need to ensure that your audience increases and your message is heard, including:

- Setting up your business
- Finding a brand that fits
- Getting more bookings
- Polishing your style
- Discovering God's plan for your business

An extensive resource section containing a sample contract, media interviewing tips, fee schedules, checklists, and much more, makes *The Ultimate Speaker's Guide* an essential toolkit you'll use time and again.

Praise for the book:

Whether you're new to speaking to promote the message God has given you or have been doing it for a while, you'll find a wealth of practical help in *The Ultimate Speaker's Guide.* Kathy's experience as a speaker and trainer fills a void in resources for Christian speakers.

— LIN JOHNSON, Write-to-Publish conference director

NOTES

1 *Oxford University Press*, Lexico.com, v. "Well-being," accessed September 13, 2021, https://www.lexico.com/en/definition/well-being.

2 *Blue Letter Bible*, KJV search results for "rest," accessed September 13, 2021, http://blb.sc/000xBA.

3 "What is soul care & why does it matter?" *Potters Inn* (blog), November 14, 2019, https://www.pottersinn.com/what-is-soul-care-1/2019/g9ei73spsc2apsyhdazjtqp9jtbw35/.

4 Tracy Winkler, Facebook comment on a post by the author, October 6, 2020, https://www.facebook.com/kathycarltonwillis/posts/10158520385769876

5 A. J. Swoboda, *Subversive Sabbath: The Surprising Power of Rest in a Nonstop World*, (Grand Rapids: Brazos Press, a division of Baker Publishing Group, 2018).

6 J.D. Greear, "How Do We Find Spiritual Rest?" *The Gospel Project*, July 25, 2013, https://www.gospelproject.com/how-do-we-find-spiritual-rest/.

7 *Blue Letter Bible*, KJV search results for "strength," accessed September 13, 2021, http://blb.sc/00DReN.

8 *Merriam-Webster*, s.v. "Curb," accessed September 13, 2021, https://www.merriam-webster.com/dictionary/curb/.

9 *Dictionary.com*, "What doesn't kill you, makes you stronger," accessed September 13, 2021, https://www.dictionary.com/e/slang/what-doesnt-kill-you-makes-you-stronger/

10 Life, Repurposed Community, May 12, 2021, Facebook, https://www.facebook.com/groups/liferepurposed/posts/474057240569524

11 "Strength training: Get stronger, leaner, healthier," Mayo Clinic, accessed September 13, 2021, https://www.mayoclinic.org/healthy-lifestyle/fitness/in-depth/strength-training/art-20046670.

12 Katey Davidson, "14 Benefits of Strength Training," *Healthline*, August 16, 2021, https://www.healthline.com/health/fitness/benefits-of-strength-training#benefits/.

13 Davidson, "14 Benefits of Strength Training."

14 Davidson, "14 Benefits of Strength Training."

15 Davidson, "14 Benefits of Strength Training."

16 Davidson, "14 Benefits of Strength Training."

17 "What Is Proprioception?" WebMD, accessed September 13, 2021, https://www.webmd.com/brain/what-is-proprioception/.

18 "The most inspiring Coco Chanel quotes to live by," *Vogue*, August 16, 2018, https://www.vogue.com.au/fashion/news/the-most-inspiring-coco-chanel-quotes-to-live-by/image-gallery/b1cb17be7e20734d0b255fbd5a478ed4/.